By the same author

1660 The Year of Restoration
Prince Rupert of the Rhine
Restoration England
A Royal Family

ANDRÉ SIMON

Patrick Morrah

ANDRÉ SIMON

Gourmet and wine lover

Constable · London

First published in Great Britain 1987
by Constable and Company Limited
10 Orange Street London WC2H 7EG
Copyright © 1987 by Patrick Morrah
Set in Linotron Plantin 11pt by
Rowland Phototypesetting Limited
Bury St Edmunds, Suffolk
Printed in Great Britain by
St Edmundsbury Press Limited

British Library CIP data
Morrah, Patrick
André Simon
1. Simon, André L.   2. Gourmets
– France – Biography
I. Title
641.013'0924   TX637

ISBN 0 09 467410 8

Four of the five children born to
André and Edith Simon are still living,
and to them this book is dedicated.

To Jeanne Rouyer Guillet
To Sister Marcelle of Jesus, ODC
To the Rev Peter Simon, SJ
To Sister Madeleine Simon
Also to the memory of André Simon *fils*,
and to his widow, Jan

Contents

Illustrations

Foreword

ANDRÉ SIMON wrote so much, and so much of what he wrote was, in one way or another, of an autobiographical nature, that any biography must be based to a large extent on his own writings. In the following pages I have made extensive use, with copious quotations, of his various books, and in particular of his two works of direct autobiography, *By Request* (1957) and *In the Twilight* (1969). These two books contain complete bibliographies of the numerous works published under his name. The titles of books by other authors which I have had occasion to use are mentioned in my text. I have therefore not found it necessary to include a bibliography of my own.

André, born in 1877, lived until 1970, dying in his ninety-fourth year. In the case of a man who died so recently it is inevitable that a great deal of any account of his life should be made up of personal reminiscences. I myself knew him from about 1955 onwards, but there are many people still alive who knew him much better. From them I have received unfailing help and co-operation, and I should like here to record my thanks.

First and foremost come the members of his family. André left five children, and the four survivors have been most generous in providing me with memories of their father and in lending me relevant documents. Their names are given in my dedication. I should also most especially like to mention his daughter-in-law Jan Simon, widow of his elder son. Mme Simon was living until recently at Little Hedgecourt, André's old home in Sussex. She received me most graciously there, and was assiduous in sorting out for me a wealth of letters and papers without which this book could never have been written.

Hugo Dunn-Meynell, executive director of the International Wine and Food Society, has been at my elbow throughout and has helped not only with his own reminiscences but with the many documents and pictures in the possession of the Society.

Hugh Johnson, author of *The World Atlas of Wine* and other authoritative works on the juice of the grape, who was particularly close to André in his later years, has helped me with recollections and with the loan of valuable correspondence. Among the present generation of wine writers I have also had help from Cyril Ray, Julian Jeffs QC and Pamela Vandyke Price.

George Rainbird, Michael Broadbent and Anthony Berry gave me many details and were indefatigable in writing out notes for my benefit. So was Mrs Arthur Rothwell (Joy Fontes), an especially close friend of André towards the end. Dr Walter Somerville, his personal physician, was most generous in giving me his time and telling me about the last days of André and Edith Simon. Mr and Mrs Victor Webb, founders of the Rhineland branch of the Wine and Food Society, and Frank Thorpy, pioneer of the Society in New Zealand, have lent me invaluable assistance. Patrick Forbes, a leading authority on champagne, helped me in the matter of the history of this wine which played so prominent a part in André's career. G. A. Hepworth and Julian Symons have provided useful information.

My publisher, Benjamin Glazebrook of the firm of Constable, has given me continuous encouragement, reinforced with some bottles of claret worthy of André Simon himself.

Finally I should like to mention Mrs E. L. Plant, who has typed the whole book with her usual efficiency.

To all these, and any others whom I may have omitted, I record my deepest gratitude. My debt to them is great.

Brighton, 1986   Patrick Morrah

1

Young Parisian

T HE International Wine and Food Society, Britain's most
widespread gastronomical association, has a pleasant
liking for anniversaries, and even before it asserted its 'international' status it had a habit of holding one of its dinners on
14 July. The choice of France's national day was a compliment not only to acknowledged French pre-eminence in the
pleasures of the table but also to the French element in the
origin of the Society in the person of its founder, André
Louis Simon.

Personally I was never very keen on this particular function. I had qualms about the date, which has always seemed
to me an occasion for mourning rather than celebration. On
one occasion, however, I decided to attend the dinner, and I
salved my conscience by means of a note on my application
for tickets, to the effect that my presence should not be taken
as indicating approval of the deplorable events of 1789.

It was not a particularly witty comment; nor was it intended to be. And I did not for a moment suppose that it
would come to the attention of the august founder-President
himself. I might have realised that few details of any kind
concerning the Society were sufficiently trivial to escape his
personal interest. At any rate he was vastly amused. He
quoted my stipulation when I presented myself on arrival for
the dinner (it was at the London Zoo's restaurant), and I
heard him chuckling over it to other guests during the
evening.

I had in fact touched a chord in the core of his inmost being. All through his long life André Simon, Anglophil though he was and a domiciled Londoner for nearly seventy years, remained a patriotic Frenchman; he served the French Republic in the field, and would willingly have died in its defence against a foreign enemy. But all the time his spiritual allegiance was to an older France, the pre-revolutionary France of the Bourbon-Capetian kings which had for centuries led the way in moulding the grace and culture of western Christian civilisation. Talleyrand is said to have declared that those who had not lived before 1789 did not know how pleasant life could be. André was born a century too late to endorse that sentiment at first hand, but it accorded with his deepest feelings.

Those feelings were imbued in him in childhood. As he records in his autobiography, *By Request*, his father, Ernest Simon, had been in his youth a *Zouave Pontifical*, a soldier of the Pope, in those last days of the Papacy's temporal monarchy before, in 1870, revolutionary forces compelled Pius IX to become the Prisoner of the Vatican. Such young Frenchmen, romantics of good family, were almost by definition as royalist as they were Catholic; they looked back nostalgically to their country's old tradition of centuries, a tradition the Revolution had never succeeded in destroying. To them St Louis, rather than Napoleon Bonaparte, was the embodiment of *la gloire de la France*. And André Simon was very much his father's son.

When their papal world collapsed about their ears, some of the *Zouaves Pontificaux* were incorporated in the French Army under the name of *Volontaires de l'Ouest*. Among them was Ernest Simon, though it would appear that he did not pursue his military career for long after 1871. He was a talented artist, and he followed his bent as a painter in water-colours. But his political and religious principles in no way changed, and he took his place at the centre of a group of fervently Catholic royalists in Paris. It was through this group that André was in due course to procure his first employment.

The family was Parisian on both sides, and it was in Paris, close to the Boulevard St Germain, that André was born on the last day of February 1877. Shortly afterwards the Simon home in the Rue Taranne had to be pulled down to make way for the widening of the boulevard, but Ernest Simon built a new house in the Rue Coëtlogon in the same district, and here André spent most of his childhood and adolescence. But the family had another house at Carolles in Normandy, on the Baie du Mont St Michel between Granvilles and Avranches, where they spent the summer; and it was here that the boy, at the age of seven or thereabouts, had a serious accident which to some extent affected his development. When he came to write *By Request* he had no recollection of the nature of what happened. All he could remember was that his spine was badly damaged, that he had to stay at Carolles with his mother when the rest of the family went back to Paris, and that he was strapped down in a rubber cast for a year and had to wear surgical stays for another year. Eventually he made a complete recovery, but there was a prolonged period when he was unable to run about or play games with his brothers and friends. All he could do was read, and this he did avidly. It was the beginning of his lifelong love of literature.

It must have been towards 1890 that he was able to resume the normal process of growing up. He was once more in the company of his five brothers and one sister, all of them leading a happy existence together in Paris; yet his accident had exacted its toll. He himself tells us that it had made him 'feel rather odd', in some indefinable way different from others of his own age, and that he suffered for many years from self-consciousness. He did not stutter, but 'just dried up'; the right word would not come at the right moment, and he found conversation difficult. But this phase passed; there was certainly nothing shy or self-conscious about the jovial and friendly extrovert that he became.

For those of us who remember only the venerable figure of comparatively recent days, at once genial and dignified, his stately bearing tempered by the sparkle of his smile and the *bonhomie* that enveloped his whole being, it is not easy to link the young André Simon with the frivolous Paris of the Naughty Nineties. And in truth the link was tenuous. The raffish, raucous life that represented the last flamboyant flourish of the *belle époque* did not extend much beyond Montmartre. Over the Seine, on the *rive gauche* where the Simons had their home, there was a different world, equally exotic but intellectual and aesthetic rather than riotous, the world of Renoir and Matisse rather than of Plon-Plon and La Belle Otero, the Closerie des Lilas rather than Maxim's. The river was the frontier, and the two worlds hardly mixed. André remembered his mother announcing that the family would not wait dinner for his eldest brother, Jacques, because *'il est allé à l'autre côté de l'eau'*. *L'eau* was not the English Channel but the Seine, but the gulf was almost as great. Jacques had gone into foreign territory, and there was no knowing when he would be back.

The *rive gauche* had its own separate existence, and of this the Simon family were a part. It would not appear that Ernest Simon made much of a mark in the very vital art circles that then flourished in the district, but he was a competent artist, some of whose pictures are still on the walls in the homes of his descendants. It is unlikely that his painting brought him in much money, and it is safe to assume that for his obviously comfortable circumstances he was indebted to inherited private means; but he was certainly a serious professional. The big house that he built in the Rue Coëtlogon was largely an investment; several floors were let out as flats, but of the three that the family kept for themselves a considerable portion was taken up by the father's studio. His wife too belonged to the art world; her father, Emile Dardoize, *Grandpère Dardoize* as André remembered him, was a landscape painter who was associated with the founders of the Paris Salon.

There was, however, a third world in the Paris of those days: one that bridged the other two. This was the world of gastronomy, and first and foremost of wine. Champagne was of the essence of the *belle époque*, and champagne indeed was to play a predominant part in the career of André Simon. But there was subtler, more sophisticated, more intellectual drinking as well. This was the age when the last great vintages of pre-phylloxera claret were coming to their splendid maturity, and these magnificent wines were drunk and discussed at many a hospitable table in Paris. The greatest experts on wine may have been found in Bordeaux or Beaune, but the capital of France, then as at other times, was accepted as the gastronomical capital of the world.

It would not appear that wine played a particularly important part in the life of Simon *père*. He was, however, a reasonably prosperous Parisian of cultured taste, and there can be little doubt that fine vintages frequently graced his table. Certainly he had friends in the wine trade, some of them in influential positions; it was to one of these that André was to owe his induction into the realms of the higher gastronomy to which he was to devote his life. In the meantime we may assume that the young Simons were brought up to appreciate the pleasures of civilised drinking from an early age.

André's first employment had no connection with wine. As he grew up the question of what he was to do in life naturally arose. Ernest Simon might be in comfortable circumstances, but they were not comfortable enough to enable his sons to live lives of leisured ease. André, the second of the six, felt himself eclipsed by Jacques, his elder brother by a little over a year. Besides being a painter of promise, Jacques passed all his examinations with flying colours and was destined for a military career. His godfather the Marquis de Beaufort, a former officer in the Zouaves Pontificaux, had made himself responsible for the boy's schooling, and he was now to go to St Cyr, the French military academy. André had spent what he described as 'six not very happy years' at Le Petit Séminaire Notre Dame des Champs. His childhood accident and its aftermath had left him lacking in the confidence needed for examinations; he failed his *baccalauréat*, and seemed unqualified for any of the professions that a young man of good family might be expected to enter.

Nor was a career in the fine arts on the cards. The third brother, Roger, was the musician of the family; the fourth, Maxime, a budding painter like Jacques. André had no musical ear, and could not draw a straight line even with a ruler. To suggest that he had no artistic sensibilities would be wrong. One who was to bring the business of good living to such a pattern of aesthetic excellence had them in abundance. But, to his own regret, the visual and auditory arts were outside his range. What was he to do?

He made his own decision. The same trouble that had hampered him in passing examinations had at least implanted in him a devotion to the printed word, and he decided that he would like to be a journalist. His ever indulgent father was ready to help, and here once more the traditionalist heritage played its part. Another of Ernest Simon's old colleagues from the days of the papal army was one Petit de Meurville, now a literary critic on the Paris *Figaro*, who at the request of his former comrades in arms had founded a journal to keep alive the Catholic and royalist causes they had at heart. It had the rather cumbersome title *L'Avant-Garde, Gazette Bi-mensuelle des Zouaves Pontificaux*. It was, or had been until now, a one-man show, but the editor agreed to accept the young journalistic aspirant as his assistant. 'Petit de Meurville was the editor-in-chief', André tells us; 'he wrote the editorials and anything else that was worth reading. I was the staff, a trainee jack-of-all-trades.'

André started work in January 1894, a month or so before his seventeenth birthday. He scanned the newspapers, picking out items of royalist interest and anything that his editor might wish to reproduce. He watched the printing and helped in the type-setting when allowed to do so; in his own words 'making myself useful or a nuisance in turn, learning the tricks of the trade, and thoroughly enjoying the sticky smell of printer's ink.'

It was a small step in the development of a long and fruitful literary career. But it was nothing more than a tentative apprenticeship, with nothing permanent in view. When the house in the Rue Coëtlogon was closed for the summer, André's assistant editorship came to an end and he went with the rest of the family to Carolles.

That August holiday of 1894 was, nevertheless, to have a far more momentous influence on the life of André Simon than had his introduction to the world of journalism. It was to take him for the first time to the country which was to be his home for nearly three-quarters of a century, and to lead him in the near future to another development which had an even more important effect on his life.

2

Hymen, Ares and Dionysus

THERE was as yet no decision on a permanent career. André had enjoyed his introduction to journalism, but his father still had ideas of putting him into commerce. He showed promise as a linguist, and with trade prospects in view he had been attending evening classes in English, Spanish and Russian. So when the family went to Carolles in the early summer of 1894 Ernest Simon had the idea that it would be good for his seventeen-year-old son to spend a few weeks in England and improve his English. Few preparations were necessary. There was no passportery in those comparatively unbureaucratic days; any Englishman or Frenchman who wanted to cross the Channel just boarded a steamer and went. So it was with André Simon. He was given 200 francs (about £8 in English money at that time), with instructions to return home when it was spent. He sailed from St Malo, the whole of his belongings in a Gladstone bag, and arrived at Southampton at the end of May for his first glimpse of England.

Such arrangements as were made for the young traveller were the work of Constant Bricourt, organist at the parish church of St Servan, near St Malo, and his wife Marthe, who was Mme Simon's sister. Oncle Bricourt knew some of the captains of channel steamers, and it was in the house of one of these, Captain Leonard Coombs, that André was given a lodging. Soon after his arrival he wrote a grateful letter to Tante Marthe which has rather curiously survived. It is full of enthusiasm for her kindness and for the hamper she has sent him. '*Chère tante*,' it begins, '*Cent et cent mille fois mercis à toi comme à maman pour la bourriche et ta lettre*' and it continues with ecstatic praise of '*le pâté merveilleux*', the chocolate, and the other dainties contained. The letter may rank as the first known gastronomic commentary from the pen of André Simon.

Accommodation in the Coombs household was adequate if hardly luxurious. More interesting contacts soon followed. Oncle Bricourt had asked his parish priest to write to Canon Scannell, of St Joseph's Catholic church, Southampton, with the request that he would keep an eye on the boy's welfare, and André was armed with his letter. When he presented it, the canon told him that most of his parishioners were poor Irish dockers, but he undertook to introduce him to the only two Catholic families who occupied a social position in the town roughly equivalent to that of the Simons.

The richer of these two families consisted only of Mrs George Dunlop, an elderly Frenchwoman who was the widow of the head of a firm of shipping and forwarding agents, and her son Archibald, now in his thirties and in charge of the business. The second household bore a name very similar to André's own. Its head was Henry Bond Symons, a retired railway engineer who had married twice and was the father of twelve children. The elder members of this brood had left the family home, but three remained. They were Isabel, a little older than André, Gordon about his own age, and Edith who was fifteen.

Isabel, André wrote later with unwonted waspishness, 'was dark, plain and plain silly; her French was abominable.' Edith, on the other hand, was fair and bright, and spoke French without trace of an English accent; both sisters had been to a finishing convent school at Angers. The younger 'had silky, wavy, auburn hair, eyes that were blue, tender and true, a clear complexion, and two tantalizing little dimples whenever she smiled, and she smiled quite a bit.'

If it was not love at first sight, it was something very close to it. 'I knew,' recorded the happy lover more than sixty years later, 'almost from the first time when I spoke to her, and in French, of course, that I never would care for anybody else.'

Such teenage resolutions of lifelong devotion are nothing very much out of the ordinary. In the normal course of events it might have been expected that the romantic young French-man would go home, as arranged, when his money was spent, and that after an initial period of ardent correspon-dence the love of a lifetime would gradually fade into fond and sentimental recollection. André Simon, however, was a singularly determined youth, and one exceptionally constant in his affections. He was deeply in love, and so evidently was Edith. One thing was certain in his mind; he was not going back across the Channel as soon as the fifty francs he had left was finished. He was going to stay as close to Edith as was humanly possible.

There was only one practical way to do it. He did not want to write home for more money; he preferred to get some work and earn enough to enable him to stay on in Southampton. Here the Dunlops, mother and son, were glad to help. George Dunlop and Co. were the Royal Mail Steam Packet Company's agents, and a good number of passengers crossed from Le Havre to sail from Southampton in the Royal Mail liners to the West Indies and South America. There were plenty of odd jobs that a willing French-speaking lad could do. 'This meant that on sailing days I could be, and indeed I was, most useful and very busy, helping French and other Continental passengers through the Customs, or finding a stray piece of luggage, or changing some of their money. On other days I was the office boy, running errands, calling and queueing for bills of lading, certificates of origin, and so on.

So I remained at Southampton, without asking for a single franc to be sent to me from Paris, all the time improving my knowledge of ships and shipping, of docks and dockers, and of the ways of men in general.'

The course of true love seemed to be running remarkably smoothly. There was perhaps some friction with Isabel; it is difficult to account otherwise for André's ill-natured comments on her. But clearly the Symons parents had no objection to an eventual match. André was making himself as popular in Southampton as he always did everywhere. He made a number of friends and led a modestly gay social life, playing lawn tennis and going on sailing trips in that summer of 1894 and attending dinners and dances when the winter came.

Then came a totally unexpected blow. Simon *père* had always taken an artistic interest in the Near East, and he had gone off to Egypt to paint; there, in April 1895, he died suddenly from sunstroke. He was forty-seven years old.

The happy life in Southampton thus came to an abrupt end. André's mother sent him a cable asking him to return at once to Paris, and he embarked the same night after saying goodbye to Edith, to Canon Scannell and to some others of his friends. Archibald Dunlop gave him the money for his fare home, with a little extra thrown in.

One last incident deserves to be mentioned, as it added to André's knowledge of human nature. He himself remembered it two generations later.

Walking disconsolately in the street on that day, he ran into one of his new friends, George Spencer. He told him what had happened, and George mumbled something about being sorry and moved on. André set him down as an unfeeling brute. But at 11.30 p.m. when he went miserably to board the night steamer for his dreary voyage to Le Havre, he found George Spencer awaiting him. He tried to thank his friend for coming to see him off, but George just pushed him

up the gangway and followed him on board. After the chance
meeting earlier in the day he had gone straight home to pack,
bought a ticket to Paris, and now insisted on going the whole
way with André so that he would not have a solitary journey
home.

After his father's death the question of André's future
career became imperative. There was no great cause for
worry. A youth so adaptable, and so willing to turn his hand
to anything that might come along, was not likely to remain
long without employment. And as always there were his
father's influential friends to give him a helping hand. Ernest
Simon evidently had a gift for friendship, a gift which was
abundantly inherited by his second son. In the old days of
1870 one of his Zouave colleagues had been the Marquis de
Beaufort, who had later stood godfather to his eldest son, and
in the Volontaires de l'Ouest one of his subordinates had
been the marquis's cousin, the young Comte Guy de
Polignac. The Polignacs were among France's oldest families, tracing their ancestry back to the Carolingian era. Over
the centuries they had evolved into a number of branches;
Comte Guy's father, the Marquis de Polignac, was the head
of one of the senior among them. What was important from
the Simon point of view was that Guy had in 1879 married
into one of the great champagne houses. His bride was the
daughter of the redoubtable Veuve Pommery, one of those
forceful ladies who have played so notable a part in the
development of the champagne industry.

Mme Pommery, having built up the firm of Pommery et
Greno into one of the most prosperous of the champagne
houses, with a particular influence on the English market,
had died in 1890. Her son Louis became the head of the firm,
but closely associated with him were his brother-in-law and
sister, now the Marquis and Marquise de Polignac.

The Marquis de Beaufort had taken Jacques Simon,
Ernest's eldest son, under his wing; and as soon as he heard

of his old friend's death he approached his Polignac cousin to see if he could help one of the other Simons in some similar way. Guy promptly wrote to Mme Simon offering to give one of her sons a start in life with Pommery et Greno.

The opportunity went naturally to André, the second son. He was delighted, and accepted with his usual enthusiasm, expressing himself ready to repay the kindness of the Polignacs by putting his heart into any job they could give him. There was, however, one drawback. Like every young Frenchman André was bound to do a three-year stint of military service, and in the normal course of events this would be due to start in 1897, when he reached the age of twenty. It would be a pity to embark on an apprenticeship in the wine trade and then have to interrupt it just as he was beginning to master the essentials.

The solution came from the usual source. Another of his father's old friends was Général Deloye, Directeur de l'Artillerie at the Ministère de la Guerre in Paris, who had no difficulty in arranging for André to begin his service at once so that he could give his whole attention to champagne from the age of twenty-one. The Polignacs were quite happy with the arrangement, and André became a gunner under instruction at Vincennes with the 13me Régiment d'Artillerie.

His first experience of army life, 'three years of the most unmilitary service that ever was', was not arduous. Training at Vincennes lasted only three months, and then Général Deloye arranged for him to be posted to the Ecole Militaire in Paris, where he was given a job on the staff of the *Revue d'artillerie*. It was *L'Avant-Garde* over again. The *Revue d'artillerie* was the official publication sent to every gunner officer, and André's main task was to read through French and foreign periodicals in search of items of artillery interest, and anything he found he submitted to the editor of the *Revue* for approval. He also did plenty of proof-reading, and he was soon promoted and entrusted with the final make-up, seeing each issue through the press.

It was work that he had come to love, and he was perfectly happy. And better than all this was that he had free time at weekends. There could have been no greater boon.

The Symonses had moved from Southampton to London, living in Brixton which was then a pleasantly rural suburb. Every Saturday afternoon when he could afford it (and one senses that he usually managed to) André changed out of uniform in time to catch the night boat train from the Gare du Nord. French third-class carriages in those days consisted of straight-backed seats of hard wood, but this did not matter to André. What did matter was that he was able to get to Brixton in time for Sunday breakfast with Edith and her family. On Sunday night he embarked on the return journey in time to report to the Ecole Militaire for duty on Monday morning.

So the three years passed pleasantly enough. On the very day that he was discharged from the Army André travelled to Rheims and presented himself at the offices of Pommery et Greno, ready to begin his apprenticeship. And on 17 October 1900, with the blessing of both families, he and Edith Symons were married at the Church of Corpus Christi in Brixton. André was twenty-three years old and Edith twenty-one.

The first illustration in *By Request* (if one excepts the frontispiece) is inscribed 'Newly Wed: October 1900'. It is clearly not a wedding-day picture, as it was taken by a Paris photographer; nor is Edith in the bridal gown she must surely have worn. But André, leaning proudly over his wife's chair, looks the model of an elegant bridegroom, immaculately dressed as he is in frock-coat with high collar and white stock. His face has the charm that always characterised him, with his fresh and open smile; the crinkly hair which looked so attractive when it had turned white is a conspicuous feature.

Edith, likewise elegantly dressed in the style of the turn of the century, seems a trifle solemn as she looks out on the world; hers is a determined face, and one feels at once that she is eminently capable of taking on the cares of matrimony and of guiding her husband through all the vicissitudes that may face them in the life that awaits them both. It is hardly a beautiful face, but one whose charm and good humour match those of her bridegroom.

From this picture one turns inevitably to the last in the same book, a photograph taken at the Dorchester in London on 17 October 1950, just fifty years later. Here a genially dignified André, with expanse of white waistcoat and gleaming gold watch-chain, holds the hand of a charmingly silver-haired Edith as, in glistening evening gown, she wields an imposing sword to cut a golden-wedding cake of majestic proportions. Now there is no doubt of Edith's smile, which echoes André's own. They are manifestly the same couple, mellowed into the grace and tranquillity of old age by half a century of exceptionally felicitous companionship.

At Rheims André and Edith took a small flat in the Rue Vauthier-le-Noir, a mile from the Caves Pommery where André started work at seven in the morning in summer and eight in winter. He tells us himself that he *walked* to work and back for lunch; an old friend who knew him in those days, however, recorded that more often than not he *ran* most of the way through sheer *joie de vivre*. His working day ended at six p.m. in summer and seven in winter. His salary was two hundred francs a month, hardly princely; but on this he and Edith were able to drink wine at all meals and to employ a good maid at twenty-five francs a month. They were ideally happy.

This first phase of André's service with Pommery did not,

however, last very long. He remained for some two years at Rheims, working with zest and learning everything he could about the champagne business. Quite evidently he gave satisfaction.

Guy de Polignac died in 1901, but the Marquise did not forget her husband's protégé. A year later she invited André and Edith to dine with her, and at the dinner table she made him a proposition. Pommery's chief agent in London, Lucien Loffet, was getting on in years and would soon be retiring. As André had an English wife, suggested the Marquise, he might like to go to the London office as one of Loffet's assistants, with every prospect of quick promotion when the expected vacancy occurred.

The suggestion was not entirely welcome to André; but, as he wrote later, 'I dared not tell the Marquise that my wife, although English, had married me to live in France, which she loved.' The offer, however, was really an excellent one, with better pay immediately and the likelihood of early advancement. As for Edith, whatever she may have thought about a return to England, she would never have made difficulties about a move that would further her husband's career. So the offer was gratefully accepted.

Thus André once more fell on his feet, as he had a habit of doing. All his life he was a favourite of fortune, but it was not simply luck. His sunny nature and his happy-go-lucky attitude to life, together with his readiness to give always of his best, could be given equal credit.

−3−

Wine and the Written Word

THERE is no wine like champagne. A trite observation perhaps; but the fact needs emphasising. For since the discovery that it is possible to produce a first-class sparkling white wine by encouraging a second fermentation in the bottle other districts of France, and other countries too, have developed similar methods in an attempt to make a wine like champagne. None has succeeded. This is not to say that good and pleasant sparkling beverages have not anywhere been produced. But not one has that peculiar, indescribable vital quality that distinguishes the first and greatest of the kind. Champagne stands alone.

Yet, historically speaking, champagne as we know it today is not a venerable product. Wine has indeed been made, as it has in most French districts, in the lovely valley of the Marne since the dawn of European civilisation; but before the seventeenth century it could boast no great distinction. There was white wine of fair quality, produced from white grapes, limited in quantity and kept for local consumption. The Marne valley, close to the Belgian border, is too far north for the production of a great red wine, which requires black grapes scorched by the sun so that their skins permeate the juice with their redness. Today, as a result of technical improvements, a limited quantity of reasonably good red wine is produced in Champagne; but in earlier times the nearest approach to a red would appear to have been what the French call a *vin gris*, a 'grey wine', not white but lacking in colour.

The revolution came in the second half of the seventeenth century. It was almost alone among revolutions in that its effects were entirely beneficial, bringing an immeasurable addition to the sum total of human happiness. From small beginnings in the north-east corner of France came the most inspiriting, most joy-giving beverage that has ever made glad the heart of man.

The development of sparkling champagne from the still wines of the Marne valley was the work, almost exclusively, of one man, and that man a simple Benedictine monk. It is a pity that we know so little for certain about Dom Pérignon of Hautvilliers Abbey; but it is not at all surprising. He was a retiring, unambitious lay brother, and the last thing that would ever have occurred to him would have been to countenance any advertisement of his achievements. All he wanted was to serve God to the best of his ability with the talents that God had given him.

That these talents were of no mean order was clearly realised by the Abbot of Hautvilliers, who appointed Dom Pérignon to the important post of cellarer to the Abbey before his thirtieth birthday. The cellarer was in charge of the general and financial administration of the monastery, and no further evidence is needed of the efficiency with which the young monk carried out his manifold duties than the fact that he held the post for forty-seven years till his death in 1715. His speciality, however, lay in the making of wine; and here he proved himself a genius.

The Abbey of Hautvilliers possessed extensive vineyards, and depended for its maintenance and its revenues largely on the making and selling of its wine. The better the wine the bigger the sales, and to Dom Pérignon it was clearly a matter of religious duty to improve the wine to the highest pitch of perfection he could achieve.

Champagne's natural wines are distinguished by a certain

effervescence, which does not last but at its strongest can produce, without artificial aid, the temporary impression of a sparkling wine, a *vin mousseux*. To Dom Pérignon came the thought that, if this natural effervescence could be retained in the liquor and brought under control, the result would be a fully sparkling wine, the qualities of which would greatly enhance its value. He set to work with an unhurried thoroughness that was typically monastic.

His achievements in the development of sparkling champagne were fourfold. First was the sheer improvement of the local wine, in which he was hardly a pioneer. There is evidence that for at least a century the wines of Champagne had been steadily improving as the art of viticulture was mastered. There is, however, equally valid evidence that the improvement, in particular that of the wine of Hautvilliers, was redoubled during Dom Pérignon's period of office. Grapes were cultivated with new skill and understanding, and the art was developed of producing a white wine from black grapes that was far superior to the *vin gris* which was the best that Champagne had been previously able to put on the market.

Hand in hand with the enhancement of the quality of the wine went the art of blending. Dom Pérignon had a palate of exquisite sensitivity. In the Abbey vineyards grew a wide variety of grapes, and the cellarer became so conversant with their flavour that he could tell unfalteringly which should be blended with which to produce the most suitable wine. 'He could tell at once,' wrote a later monk of Hautvilliers, 'without being told, which grapes came from which vineyard, and he would say, "The wine of that vineyard must be married with the wine of that one," and never did make a mistake.'

Towards the end of his life Dom Pérignon became totally blind. So far from this adversely affecting his powers it actually accentuated them, at least so far as blending was concerned. The loss of one faculty brought intensification of another, and his palate advanced still further towards perfection.

So much for the natural wine of Champagne. When it came to what to do with this wine, how to turn the still product into a genuine *vin mousseux*, Dom Pérignon's innovations were more original. The two complementary devices that completed the creation of sparkling champagne were the bottle and the cork.

Before the seventeenth century all wine was kept in cask. Smaller receptacles made of various materials were used, but only as open decanters for taking the wine from cask to table. The cask itself was adequate for keeping still wine, but useless for preserving the effervescence which became manifest in the second fermentation. For this a vessel was needed of a hard substance which would keep the sparkle intact.

The glass wine bottle seems to have originated in England. It first appeared about the time that Dom Pérignon started his régime as cellarer of Hautvilliers Abbey; it approximated to the form of the modern wine bottle, but with a much broader base it could not be kept in the horizontal position essential for the preservation of wine over a long period. Vintage wines, however, were a later boon; in Dom Pérignon's day all wines were drunk fairly young.

When exactly the glass bottle was first used in Champagne is not known, but it was certainly during Dom Pérignon's term of office. He may not have been directly responsible for its introduction, but undoubtedly he developed it and saw the use he could make of it. The bottle would preserve the sparkle intact – provided a means could be found of sealing the opening through which the wine was to be poured.

The old cask which served as a container for wine was normally sealed with a wooden stopper bound round with hemp which had been dipped in oil. This system was continued when the first glass bottles appeared. It was considered adequate for keeping still wine, but it did not provide the hermetic seal needed to preserve effervescence.

Dom Pérignon found the solution, and this was his fourth contribution to the making of the new wine. It was another importation from abroad; the bottle came from England, the cork from Spain. According to the traditional story two Spanish monks on a journey through France put up at Hautvilliers, where their hosts noticed an unfamiliar substance with which their water gourds were sealed. They were told that it was the bark of the cork-oak tree, which had proved the ideal form of stopper. Dom Pérignon looked into the matter, and his investigations convinced him that he had stumbled on the very device for which he had been searching. He ordered a consignment of the Spanish cork on behalf of the Abbey, and succeeded in hermetically sealing his bottles and thus preserving the sparkle in the wine.

And so, after some thirty years of work and study, the greatest of sparkling wines was born. The date is usually given as about 1690.

Such is the generally accepted story. It has not gone unchallenged; and its most formidable challenger, perhaps, has been none other than André Louis Simon himself.

André yielded to no man in his veneration for the memory of Dom Pérignon, but as a scholar and historian of wine he was unwilling to give him credit to which, in his opinion, the historical evidence did not entitle him. With his vast erudition he was able to unearth evidence that the principle of using a second fermentation to preserve sparkle had been understood before Dom Pérignon's time and that bottles and corks had been used for this purpose before the great cellarer was born. In his little book *Champagne*, published in 1934, he writes categorically: 'Dom Pérignon did not discover, invent or create sparkling Champagne. He never claimed to have done so, nor did any of his contemporaries claim any such honour for him.'

Yet even on the subject of champagne André Simon has no prescriptive right to the last word. Thirty-three years after he made his pronouncement Patrick Forbes, armed with a weight of research which even André could not equal, produced his monumental work on the province and its wine, also entitled simply *Champagne*. In it Mr Forbes goes into every detail of Dom Pérignon's career and achievements, and his conclusions approach far closer to the traditional version than to the more sceptical Simon verdict contained in the earlier book. He shows that, whatever may be the truth concerning the various inventions that went to make up the first true sparkling wine, it was Dom Pérignon who harmonised them into a perfect whole, and the result was the modern wine called champagne. His final verdict deserves quotation:

> Perhaps, one day, the Hautvilliers archives that were lost during the Revolution will turn up in some dusty attic and help to disentangle truth from legend. If that day should come, I am confident that it will be found that Dom Pérignon deserves an even higher place in the esteem of wine-lovers than he enjoys already.

One feels that André would not have disagreed. The difference between his views and those of Patrick Forbes was one of emphasis rather than of fact. Dom Pérignon's eminence remains supreme after all the controversies have been dissected; he lacks only formal canonisation to be proclaimed the Patron Saint of Wine, or at least of Champagne.

In the development of sparkling champagne there was still a long way to go. Refinement of the process of production went on continuously throughout the eighteenth century until it resulted in what may be regarded as the golden age of champagne in the second half of the nineteenth.

It was in this period that the great champagne houses whose names are so familiar to wine-lovers of today grew up. Pride of place among the early producers is given by Mr Forbes to a great French family, the Brularts of Sillery. Of the firms that now exist, the pride of the two great champagne towns Rheims and Epernay, the first was Ruinart, followed by Moët et Chandon (now the largest), Lanson, Louis Roederer, Clicquot (the house of the famous widow), Heidsieck, Perrier-Jouët, Mumm and Bollinger.

Pommery et Greno came comparatively late on the scene, and the firm's earliest years were unmemorable. Founded by two Rheims business men in 1836, it at first specialised in the still red wines of the Marne valley. But in 1858 Pommery died. His partner Greno was in poor health, and was only too glad to yield the dominant place in the partnership to Pommery's widow, who quickly transformed the whole outlook of the firm and made it a power to be reckoned with.

Louise Pommery never attained the fame of her counterpart of half a century earlier, the great Veuve Clicquot, and there was in fact not much resemblance between them. 'There was really nothing whatever that these two remarkable Frenchwomen had in common,' wrote André Simon, 'except that they each married a nonentity and made his name illustrious.' But in her capacity and acumen Mme Pommery was a comparable character. She was thirty-nine when she took over the work of her dead husband; she died in 1890 at the age of seventy-one, still in complete control of the firm of Pommery et Greno, now generally known just as Pommery. In those thirty-two years, in the words of Patrick Forbes, 'she transformed the modest little business into one of the largest and most prosperous, and certainly the most spectacular, of all the champagne firms.'

Mme Pommery had two principal objectives. First she concentrated her attention on sparkling champagne, setting aside the still variety. Secondly she set herself to conquer the English market.

This market was expanding rapidly. Champagne has always sold well in England, but sales increased enormously with the development of a dry wine. Up to the middle of the nineteenth century all sparkling champagne was artificially sweetened with sugar. The French preferred it this way, drinking it mainly as a dessert wine. The English, however, already had a wine for this purpose, the fortified port on which the long-established alliance with Portugal had conferred official favour, deliberately fostered to the detriment of the less popular trade with France. Port was the beverage of the great imbibers of the eighteenth century and early nineteenth, the three-bottle men who sat for hours over their after-dinner potations. The English connoisseur did not want a new dessert wine.

Towards 1850 astute makers of champagne came to realise that if a dry wine were developed it could revolutionise the English market. Developed it was; and sales to England soared. English wine-drinkers were the fathers of dry champagne, which up to the present time has kept its pre-eminence in this country. Sweet champagne retains its popularity in its native land. On this side of the Channel the dry variety reigns supreme – a wine that can be drunk with any kind of food, at virtually any hour of the day or night; a wine that is equally at home as an *apéritif*, throughout a meal, and at every sort of convivial assembly.

All this took place during the early days of Mme Pommery's régime, and that shrewd businesswoman was not slow to take advantage of it. Under her guidance the firm produced and perfected an excellent dry champagne, and one of the most trusted of her team of advisers, Adolphe Hubinet, was sent to London to act as her agent in selling the wine to the English. He opened an office at 24 Mark Lane, destined to be for many years the headquarters of André

Simon. By the time of Mme Pommery's death the English trade of her firm could compete with that of any of its older and larger competitors.

Mme Pommery's success in the social world was equal to her triumph in business. Elegant and charming, she moved easily in the sophisticated surroundings of the *belle époque*. The culmination of her rise in the social scale came in 1879 with the marriage of her daughter to Comte Guy de Polignac, shortly to succeed to his father's title of Marquis. It was to these two that André Simon owed his appointment to his post in the London agency. The Marquis gave him his first post with Pommery; his widow the Marquise sent him to England.

André had two superiors at 24 Mark Lane. Lucien Loffet, Hubinet's successor, was in charge of the agency, in which he had recently been joined by Frederick Thellusson, eldest son of Lord Rendlesham. The Thellussons were in origin a French family; Frederick, who had been for some years a wine merchant in London, was a discriminating gastronome and a convivial character. He and André, who was nine years his junior, quickly became firm friends.

As the Marquise had predicted, Loffet retired within a few months. Frederick Thellusson took his place, and André became Thellusson's partner, a post he held for nine years before Frederick succeeded to the Rendlesham barony on his father's death and left the firm. He and André worked in complete accord, and under his friendly guidance the younger man was able to perfect his knowledge of the champagne trade.

This period was a happy one. The firm was reaping the reward of the skill and foresight of Mme Pommery and the hard work of Hubinet and Loffet, and its English trade had been brought to a pitch of prosperity. Prices realised for the excellent vintage wines produced compared favourably with those of any of the champagne houses, and the trade in non-vintage wines flourished in proportion.

André revelled in the task he was given, which was to keep up the high level of trade already achieved, and if possible to improve it. There was plenty to do, but he was never afraid of hard work. There was, moreover, social life in abundance of the kind he loved. In *By Request* he thus describes the sort of existence it was his pleasure as well as his duty to lead:

> The champagne shipper must be out and about at all times of day and night, meeting as many different people as possible, making friends, the right kind of friends, all the time, friends who will not only like him but like his wine also, call for it, talk about it, and have his brand chosen in preference to all others, whenever the occasion or opportunity occurs. The champagne shipper must be a good mixer rather than a good salesman, neither a teetotaller nor a boozer, but able to drink champagne every day without letting it become a bore or a craving. If he be a really good champagne shipper, there will be no cause for him to call for orders: his brand, that is the champagne which he has to sell, will be the talk of the town and the fashion of the day, and wine merchants will queue up outside his office begging him to accept their orders . . .

The qualities called for were precisely those that André possessed. The quantity of champagne that he was required to drink presented no problem; all his life he was blessed with a cast-iron constitution. The zest he put into his work, and his warmth of personality, made him universally popular, and he received any amount of hospitality, both in London and in the provinces. Edith played her part, and it was an important part. She too loved the life, and her gaiety and vitality made her an admirable hostess and an always welcome guest. 'My greatest asset', wrote André, 'was to have a young, good-looking and socially-minded wife, who was a great favourite.'

In the intervals of social life she found time to present her husband with a happy and healthy family. Jeanne, the first-born, made her appearance on 22 September 1901. Another daughter, Marcelle, followed fourteen months later, and the first son, André, on 3 August 1906. The second son, Peter, was born in 1909, and Madeleine in 1912.

A year before this youngest daughter appeared, André had succeeded to the headship of the agency; he took as his partner Percy Thellusson, younger brother of Frederick, who was now Lord Rendlesham. The Simons had been living in Norbiton, but with his improved circumstances André was able to move into the bigger quarters which his growing family needed. He and Edith took a lease of a large house, No. 8 The Downs, close to Wimbledon Common.

So the early years in London passed pleasantly for the young couple – a life of pleasure and laughter as well as hard work, brightened by the antics of a lively brood of children and enlivened by limitless quantities of champagne. Who, it might well be asked, could ask for more? André could, and did. His work in selling champagne was not enough. His first love had been literature, and he still felt the urge to turn out words.

Such writing as he had already done was all in French, in the form of contributions to those journals for which he had worked. Although he now spoke good English, albeit with the strong French accent which he never lost, he was diffident about making any attempt to write in a foreign language, apart of course from the letters he had to compose in the course of business. That he ventured to try his hand at English literature was brought about by the encouragement of one of the good friends he had now made in England, Arthur Stephen Gardiner.

Gardiner was editor of the *Wine Trade Review*; seventeen years older than André, he quickly took the young Pommery representative under his wing. The story of how André came to embark on his first book is told both in *By Request* and in his second book of autobiography, *In the Twilight*.

Talking one day to Gardiner, he lamented that he had had to give up his ambition to be a writer; he had a wife and children to support now, and all his energies must be devoted to selling champagne. Gardiner replied: 'Nonsense! you cannot sell, any more than drink, champagne all day. If you were born a writer, the urge to write will be with you all your life, and you will never be really happy unless you write. As it happens, you could find time, I am sure, to write as well as sell champagne.' André objected that as a Frenchman he could not expect to be able to write anything that anybody in England would want to read. This time Gardiner had a practical answer. 'You are quite wrong,' he said, 'and to prove that I mean it I am quite willing to publish in the *Wine Trade Review* twelve articles on champagne, to be paid for at our usual rates.'

André jumped at the offer, and immediately began reading up all he could get hold of about the history of the wine. He knew quite a lot already, but he avidly scanned the records of Christie's, to which Gardiner introduced him, and everything he could find in the Guildhall Library, in addition to perusing back numbers of the *Wine Trade Review*. The result was that he was soon as well informed as any budding writer could be expected to be. The twelve articles, dealing with trade relations between England and Champagne from the Restoration of Charles II to the Edwardian age, duly appeared in the *Wine Trade Review* in 1904, and in the following year, through the good offices of Gardiner and to André's joy, they were published in book form as *The History of the Champagne Trade in England*.

This book never made much of a mark, and has been long

out of print. In later years André was inclined to belittle it. It was not a good book, he said, and it was poorly printed. Yet it was not without significance. It contained a considerable amount of little-known information, and its merit was indicated by the fact that André's former superior in Pommery, Lucien Loffet, paid for its private printing. It was chiefly notable, however, in that this was the first full-length work from the pen of André Simon, and its value, like that of many another such initial enterprise, lay in the lessons learned by the author from its composition. From *The History of the Champagne Trade in England* André acquired much understanding of the art of writing English, and at the same time of the first essential of the historian, the technique of research and the knowledge of where to go to find his facts. This first venture led him on to more important work.

His hurried researches had fired him with the ambition to study more extensively the history of wine and the wine trade. By its nature the champagne trade in England could not take him further back than the seventeenth century; the old still wines of the Marne Valley had not been exported to any degree. But wine in its various aspects had been part of the history not only of France but of England from early times. André set to work to produce a complete narrative as it affected the English trade up to the time when his story of champagne began.

The first book had given him an insight into the wealth of documentation that existed in the Guildhall Library, and it was there that the bulk of his research was done. But he used plenty of other sources as well, as is clear from the most cursory perusal of the work that emerged. Indeed it must be a constant source of wonder how he managed, in the midst of selling and drinking champagne and indulging in a full social life, to acquire the vast stock of knowledge that he displayed.

The first volume of *The History of the Wine Trade in England* appeared in 1906. It was published at the author's own expense, an indication that he had prospered well since crossing the Channel. The printers were Wyman and Sons, who had also been responsible for the champagne book; this time they made a better job of it. It is a handsome volume of nearly 400 pages. The cover is stamped with an elegant design showing a wine ship in full sail, the work of André's artist brother Jacques.

The title-page is followed by an elaborate dedication, set out in capital letters in the form of an inverted pyramid. 'This work', it proclaims, 'is dedicated to the cause of temperance, in no spirit of irony, but with feelings of deep conviction that a better knowledge of the history of wine in this country would promote amongst the public a greater appreciation of the virtues of wine, the more general use of which would help to check both drunkenness and teetotalism, evils which every fair-minded and temperate man cannot help deploring.'

The inscription is not free of pomposity, the pomposity of a young man sure of himself; it may even have evoked a slight shudder from the more mature André if he ever reread it in later years. It embodies, nevertheless, a heartfelt conviction to which he had come, and which he maintained to the end of his days. Wine and the good life which goes with it are among the best of God's gifts to man, an essential element of civilisation, and to abjure them is a violation of God's law, quite as bad as any misuse or excess.

As to the book itself, its writing is by any criterion an astonishing achievement. Here was a Frenchman not yet thirty, with less than five years' continuous residence in England, writing in a language not his own, yet producing a literary history of which no English academic need have been ashamed. The depth and width of research displayed are quite remarkable. *The History of the Wine Trade in England* shows mastery of a wealth of original documents in Latin, French and English; medieval Latin records are not the easiest object of study, and André was clearly a much more learned classical scholar than many people realised.

He begins his survey with the origins of wine-drinking in Britain, showing the fallacy of the popular idea that the practice began with Julius Caesar and the invaders who followed him. On the contrary, not only was the cultivation of the vine unknown in ancient Britain, but there were no commercial imports before the advent of Christianity and the first Christian missionaries in the fourth or the fifth century. Wine was essential for celebration of the Mass. It was the Catholic Church, not the Roman Empire, that originated the wine trade in Britain.

From there on André traces with unerring skill, and in lucid English, the development of the trade through the middle ages, showing how the encouragement of kings, nobles and prelates made England a wine-drinking country, with a special interest in the wines of Bordeaux, an English possession from the reign of Henry II. This first volume takes the story up to the end of the fourteenth century.

The second volume, dealing with the fifteenth and six-teenth centuries, appeared a year later, in 1907; the third, published in 1909, brought the narrative up to the end of the seventeenth century, when the champagne trade had been established in England.

Volume I was offered at 5s. a copy, the other two at 10s. They did not sell. André wrote specifically for his colleagues in the wine trade, a limited clientèle. The general reading public were not interested. Modern Great Britain, except for a restricted circle in the upper ranks of society, was a land of beer and whisky. The time had not yet come when an erudite work on wine could hope for commercial success.

Nevertheless the book remained André's favourite among all his printed works. 'There is more hard work and original information', he wrote in *By Request*, 'in these three Volumes than in all my other books.' It had, moreover, broadened his outlook. Until this time, it would appear, he had taken no particular professional interest in any wine other than champagne. Now the juice of the grape in all its aspects became of absorbing concern to him, and so it came about that his next publication, in 1912, was entitled *The Search After Claret*. He had already become a collector of rare volumes on wine, and this book consisted mainly of a facsimile reprint of some tracts which he had acquired on the wines of Bordeaux, written in the seventeenth century. André, however, contributed his own 'Notes on Claret'. Only fifty copies were printed, at the editor's expense; they were given to a selection of his friends and customers.

In the meantime, and before the publication of the third volume of *The History of the Wine Trade in England*, André had crossed the Atlantic for the first time. The trade of Pommery was expanding in South America and Melchior, Marquis de Polignac, son of André's original patrons, who was now in charge of the firm, invited him to visit its agents there and report on what changes were desirable. It was a responsible assignment and a fine chance to see lands that were new to him.

He sailed in the Royal Mail liner *Amazon* on 15 November 1907 from Southampton, and he took the opportunity to give a dinner on the night before the ship left to some of his old friends in the town where he had spent his first months in England. His guest of honour was Archibald Dunlop, the shipping agent who had befriended him by giving him odd jobs so that he could stay in the country and be near Edith Symons.

The dinner was held at the South Western Hotel, Southampton. André kept the menu, which is of interest as showing how a young man (he was just thirty), holding a subordinate position in a wine agency, was at that time able to entertain his friends:

Whitstable Natives

Tortue Claire

Rougets à la Vaucluse

Blanchailles à la Diable

Casserole de Ris de Veau à la South Western

Selle de Pré-salé Renaissance
Céleris braisés à la Moëlle
Choufleur au gratin
Pommes Dauphine et Fondantes

Sorbet au Pommery
Cigarettes Teofani

Faisan en volière

Bécassine flambée à la Fine Champagne
Panier de Pommes Paille
Salade Demi-deuil

Soufflé Palmyre

Chartreuse de Fruits à la Moderne

Bombe Alhambra
Petits Fours Parisiens

Croûte à la Baron

Dessert et Café

The wines were Amontillado sherry, Berncasteler moselle, Pommery champagne and Cockburn's port, with Gautier's brandy to follow.

André spent some six months in Argentina, Chile, Peru and Panama. He enjoyed himself thoroughly, making new friends and studying the gastronomic habits of the countries

concerned. These habits, however, were not altogether beneficial to him. In Peru he was taken seriously ill with food
poisoning, the result apparently of the local custom of eating
fish after it had passed its first youth. André's life was
momentarily in danger, but his splendid constitution,
coupled with the attentions of a good French doctor, pulled
him through. The illness took its toll, however; Edith, who
with her three children had spent the months of separation
with her mother-in-law in Paris, was shocked at her husband's appearance when she met him at Waterloo on his
return. 'My collar was three sizes too big,' he wrote, 'my
clothes did not fit, I was yellow instead of pink, and twelve
stones instead of fifteen.' She insisted on his seeing a specialist, who forbade him alcohol and recommended a diet of
Vichy water. André ignored the advice. He had more faith in
the curative powers of champagne, and was soon restored to
normal health.

André was becoming an influential figure in the wine circles
of the City of London. He was on friendly terms with
Pommery's competitors, and in 1908, on his return from
South America, he and his cronies formed the Wine Trade
Club. His friend and mentor A. S. Gardiner was elected the
first president, to hold office for a year; André became
vice-president, and in 1909 duly succeeded Gardiner as
president for the next twelve months. On giving up office in
1910 he was elected 'trustee in perpetuity'.

The Wine Trade Club had a number of homes, moving
from one to another as its membership grew, finally coming
to roost in Byward Street. It was a convivial institution,
holding luncheons and dinners at which the best of wines
were served. At a small lunch which André gave at his Mark
Lane premises, to make the final arrangements for the
move to Byward Street, he produced his last magnum of
Pommery 1889, followed by a bottle of 1868 Cockburn's

port and a glass for each guest of 1808 Denis Mounié brandy.

The club also arranged lectures, tours of vineyards, golf and cricket matches, and entertainments of various kinds, including amateur theatricals. André, to show his versatility, wrote a one-act farce, *My French Friend*, for the club to perform. It is a light-hearted triviality, in which a visitor to London outwits his English acquaintances with worldly wisdom and a magnum of champagne, and it still reads amusingly enough. It was produced at the Royal Court Theatre in February 1912.

A memorable occasion was France's first Aviation Week. André had planned an expedition for the Wine Trade Club education committee to Champagne for the vintage in September 1909. But in July of that year Louis Blériot made his epoch-making air crossing of the Channel, and aeronautics became the passion of the hour. It was decided to hold an aviation week at Bétheny, near Rheims, in August; the chief organiser was none other than André's employer Melchior de Polignac, then twenty-seven years old and an enthusiast for flying.

The occasion was too good to miss, and the expedition was advanced to August. Thirteen members of the Wine Trade Club, led of course by André Simon, went to Rheims and were royally entertained. The Marquis de Polignac was their principal host, but the various champagne houses vied with each other in hospitality. There was plenty of flying to watch, but there was even more champagne to drink, gargantuan in quantity but at the same time superb in quality. André describes one of the lunches:

. . . The fare was wonderful, and so were the wines, a Blanc de Blancs 1905 as an apéritif; an Avize 1892 with the fish course and then a Carte d'Or 1884, a pre-phylloxera, twenty-five-year-old wine, the oldest Champagne my

'students' had ever tasted, and an amazingly fresh wine for
its age – although, naturally, not violently sparkling. To
finish with a Carte d'Or 1898, more lively but mature
withal. A real treat indeed.

On the final day, 31 August, the delegates were the guests of
Heidsieck Dry Monopole at the Moulin de Verzenay, that
glorious spot with its old windmill looking down on the
Marne Valley:

. . . Year after year, day after day, visitors from all parts of
the world have come to this unique observatory and
admired the view that we admired, but there was on this
last day of August 1909 another view which, I believe, had
never been seen before and was never seen again. Upon
a long refectory table almost as long as the room, there
stood twenty-four Magnums of Dry Monopole 1892, one
magnum for each of the twenty-four men who sat
down to lunch, fourteen of us and ten others; some of them
members of the firm, others their guests . . .

One guest cheated – the youngest present. He went to the
help of the eldest, who found a magnum more than he could
drink.

Those last years of peace were a golden time for the young
agent of Pommery. But it was too good to last. In 1914 the
exploits of the German Kaiser disrupted his life as they did
those of millions of others.

-4-

Vintner in Uniform

I N August 1914 André Simon was thirty-seven years old, a prosperous wine shipper with a growing reputation and with a wife and five children. He could have continued his peaceful existence, at least for some time, with a minimum of interruption. He would not have been called up at once on the outbreak of war, and when he was he would almost certainly, in view of his age and position, have been appointed to some such organisation as one of the French purchasing commissions which were soon formed to operate in England. All he had to do was wait.

In later years he consistently played down the fact that he did nothing of the sort. In his autobiography he describes what he did do as one of the most foolish actions of his life. He had, he writes, no burning desire to die for his native country; his military experience was negligible, and he was unlikely to be of any use to the French Army. The excuse he makes for himself is that he expected for that reason to be sent back to London at once, and he emphasises that when he travelled to France he bought a return ticket.

The fact remains that no sooner had the Germans invaded Belgium, making a European war certain, than he left London to report for duty with the artillery regiment in whose ranks he had served in arms to the extent of editing a military magazine. The third of August was the eighth birthday of André *fils*, and the boy entreated his father to stay at home for his tea party; but the elder André was not to be moved. He was a Frenchman, and his plain duty was to put his services at the disposal of *la patrie*. That morning he caught the eleven o'clock boat train from Victoria.

Headquarters of the 13th Artillery Regiment were at Vincennes, and thither André repaired next day, the fateful 4 August, to queue up for an interview with the recruiting sergeant. In accordance with immemorial army custom the willing volunteer, a reservist who had already served with the regiment, albeit a gunner who had never fired a gun, found himself frustrated by military protocol. There were forms to fill up, and there was rigorous interrogation from the sergeant, who regarded him with deep suspicion and was plainly out to reject him if possible. At length the question came: what was his occupation in civilian life? André thought quickly. If he mentioned the wine trade, he reasoned, he would at once be posted to the canteen; this was not the sort of soldiering he wanted. So he fell back on his literary activities, and described himself as an *homme de lettres*. This transformed the situation. The recruiting sergeant became quite friendly and helpful. A man of letters was just what the unit wanted. André's application was accepted, and he was given an immediate job as regimental postman.

Sorting mail and licking stamps were no more congenial military occupations than would have been serving beer in a canteen bar. André felt that he was capable of serving his country in some more effective way than this; so, greatly daring, he ventured to approach the officer under whom he was serving with the suggestion that, being bilingual, he should be employed as an interpreter with one of the British Expeditionary Force units. The interview was short. The captain demanded to see André's *livret militaire*, the record of his national service. Unfortunately the *livret* stated only that he could read, write and swim. Plainly he was a liar. If the official record did not say that he could speak English, obviously he could not. So he was told not to be impertinent, and was thrown out of the office before he could explain that the record had been compiled some fifteen years earlier and that long residence in England might perhaps have brought about an improvement in his linguistic abilities.

André, as has been remarked before, was persistent in getting his way. He had decided that he wanted to be an Anglo-French interpreter, and he was not going to be put off becoming one. The military authorities, fortified with the irrefutable evidence of army records, were convinced that he was not bilingual. Very well, he would show them they were wrong. The method he decided on was ambitious, elaborate, and above all dangerous. He would write books in the two different languages, in the process defying sacred canons of military discipline.

He chose the field of biography. Disillusionment with the higher command had not yet set in among the lower ranks of the allied armies, and the heroes of the hour were General Joseph Joffre, the French commander-in-chief, and Field-Marshal Sir John French, who led the British Expeditionary Force. André set to work to produce a short life of Joffre in English and another of the British general in French.

The self-imposed task was not difficult for a practised writer of André's capacity. In the public library at Vincennes he found all the details he needed of Joffre's military career. With the aid of the voluminous reports now being published in the popular press, and a certain amount of comment by himself, he turned out a booklet just long enough to be called a biography.

André knew perfectly well that, if he asked for permission to have his work published, not only would the request be refused, but he would probably be court-martialled into the bargain. So he dispensed with any such formality, and simply sent his manuscript off to London. There, early in 1915, it was published by Simpkin Marshall, as *General Joffre: a Popular Life of the Hero of the French Nation*, at one shilling a copy. It received a 400-word review in the *Morning Post*.

Meanwhile he had quickly rattled off the kindred volume on Sir John French. This was even easier. André got hold of an issue of a London magazine which was devoted almost entirely to the BEF commander. He paraphrased and translated the articles into French, supplied the necessary padding, and the work was done. He knew the Paris publisher Lethielleux, and persuaded him to produce a paperback edition, entitled *Le Maréchal French*, at fifty centimes (fivepence).

He had not gone so far in effrontery as to put his full name on the title-page of either. The English book was 'by a French Gunner' (a 'rather inaccurate caption' was his own comment), though his initials appeared unobtrusively at the end. On the French one he went one step further by describing it on the title-page as 'par A.L.S.' Once they were published, however, all attempt at anonymity was abandoned; André applied for a second interview with his superior officer, and serenely presented him with a copy of each book as evidence that he was well enough versed in French and English to write publishable literature in both tongues.

In *In the Twilight* we read that André now felt sure that victory was in sight. The captain 'would now know that I did not lie and maybe beg my pardon'. One may take leave to doubt this assertion; he was not so innocent as that. His patent object was the very human one of making the officer look a fool, and he was prepared to risk the consequences.

The resultant explosion cannot have been unexpected. The captain 'flew into a violent rage and shouted that I must be mad'. To write and publish books without the permission of the authorities was bad enough; but for a private soldier, a regimental postman, to make critical comments on the senior generals of two armies – this was enough to rock the French military establishment to its foundations. 'I would send you to hell if I knew how to do it' was the captain's recorded comment.

This, however, was the crux of the matter; it showed that André had judged the situation shrewdly, and that his behaviour was not so suicidally demented as it appeared. For the gallant captain did *not* know how to consign his fiendish subordinate to his predestined home in the infernal regions. He could, it was true, arrange for a court-martial, with a certain verdict of guilty. But how would this affect his own career? At the best the evidence would make him look as silly as André had obviously intended; at the worst it could suggest the aiding and abetting of the culprit's crime. No, the only rational course was to get rid of this appalling subverter of army discipline before he wrecked the regiment.

It so happened that, just at this convenient moment, a circular had been sent out from the French War Office directing that a search should be made for 'other ranks' who could read, write and speak English, and who could be spared; they were to be recruited for a new military organisation known as *La Mission*, formed at Le Havre for the purpose of supplying liaison officers and interpreters to units of the BEF.

Of one thing the captain needed no convincing. Gunner Simon could be spared. So he pocketed his pride and recommended his persecutor for *La Mission*.

It was exactly the object at which André had been aiming. Once again he had got what he wanted; and he had got it by characteristically individual means.

The war now took a different course for André. At Vincennes he had been well away from the firing line, and this continued during his brief period of instruction, mainly learning about the British Army, at Le Havre. But before long he found himself in Flanders, in the hottest part of the Western Front. In April 1915 the Germans, using poison gas for the first

time, broke through the allied line at Ypres, making a gap
between the French and Canadian forces; and into this gap
the British 50th (Northumbrian) Division was thrown as
soon as it arrived in France. The fighting in the Ypres Salient
was fierce; within a week General Riddell, the divisional
commander, was killed. And it was just at this time
that André Simon was posted to the 50th Division as an
interpreter.

A certain mystery attaches to André's war service. He
himself in later years would never give details; it was always
his way to speak light-heartedly about it all, giving the
impression that he was never within distance of hostilities.
This does not accord with the few known facts. It was not, of
course, part of the duties of an interpreter to fire gun or rifle;
yet it seems certain that throughout a good deal of 1915 and
1916 he was in and out of the front line. One detail that
emerges is that in the latter year he was honoured with the
British Military Medal. The reason for the award to one who
was not even a member of the British forces evades research;
army records are of no assistance. There is no doubt that he
did indeed win it; the medal itself survives to prove this.
Neither then nor at any other time has the MM been
conferred for nothing.

His modest reticence likewise affects the conditions of his
service. He records that on moving out of the line for a rest at
Steenwoorde in May 1915 he was provided with a horse and a
batman. These are not the perquisites of a private soldier; yet
there is no indication that he was ever given a commission.
The truth would appear to be that he was attached to the
British forces in a civilian capacity, while retaining his
modest rank as a gunner in the French artillery.

He was two years with the 50th Division, during which
time that formation suffered heavy casualties in the most
gruelling of battlefields. Ypres, Poperinghe, Armentières,
Arras – the familiar names crop up in his autobiographical

books; but of his own exploits there is nothing. What he did write about was his relaxation; when out of the battle area he contrived to enjoy himself in the old familiar way. In the divisional headquarters mess he inevitably took charge of catering, and imparted what knowledge he could to the mess cooks. On 18 June 1915 came the celebration of the centenary of the Battle of Waterloo, and the mess sat down to a dinner of which the menu can have been organised by nobody but André Simon, in spite of his being a representative of the defeated side. It showed what ingenuity he was capable of putting into the titivation of army rations:

> Petite Marmite à la Thermit
>
> Saumon de Tin; A & Q Sauce
>
> Epaule d'Agneau Wellington (NZ)
> Pommes Nouvelles
> Petit Pois Poperinghois
>
> Terrine de Foie Gras aux Truffes
>   Coeurs de Laitue
>
> Macédoine de Fruit à la Quatre-Bras
>
> Canapé Saillant d'Ypres
>
> Fraises Napoléon

Likewise there could be no doubt about who procured the wines. The list consisted of Gonzalez Amontillado, Berncasteler 1904, Pommery et Greno Extra Sec, Graham's Five Crown port, and 'Waterloo Cup', whatever that may have been.

On another occasion he discovered that one of his closest friends in the wine trade, Ian Campbell of Reid, Pye and Campbell, now a captain in the Argylls, was near at hand in the Armentières sector. Looking forward to a joyful reunion, he got hold of a staff car and set off with a bottle of his best wine in each pocket. On the way he was greatly saddened to hear that Captain Ian Campbell had been killed a week earlier. He decided to go on to the forward billets and find out what he could, and there the first officer he met was his good friend. There were so many Ian Campbells in the Argylls that confusion was bound to occur from time to time. The two friends were able to enjoy their wine with the greater pleasure.

André, of course, went on writing. He had got the literary bit between his teeth, and nothing would stop him. But it was easier for him now. He was still supposed to get permission, but an official interpreter could hardly be expected to abjure the written word.

His first publication after the Joffre and French biographies was *Somewhere in Flanders*, a short guide to the history and topography of the country for the benefit of the men of the 50th Division. It appeared in the spring of 1916, and his own copy is inscribed: 'To my brave little wife, whose patience and courage have cheered and helped me so much during dreary months in Flanders, I dedicate these few notes.'

There followed the most unlikely volume that was ever to emerge from his pen – no less than a manual of instruction in Russian.

Belief in the 'Russian steamroller', the vast mass of man-power that the biggest country in the world was thought to be capable of putting into the field, was not yet shaken, and it was accepted that Germany would turn the bulk of her strength in this direction when she felt able to do so. There was talk in 1915 that British officers and men would be sent in large numbers to Archangel to help and train the Russians, and in the long and frustrating winter that followed André, 'out of sheer desperation', decided to cash in on the possibility.

He was not totally ignorant of Russian; in the days before his first trip to England he had attended evening classes in the language. But he could neither read nor speak it to any degree. This did not deter him. He wrote off to Edith asking her to get hold of any books she could on the subject. She accordingly sent him a Russian grammar and a Russian-French dictionary. These were enough. With his usual facility André turned out an elementary booklet that would help British soldiers to ask for what they wanted in the event of their being sent to Russia. This he dispatched as a gift to his old publishers, Wyman and Sons, to do what they liked with. They chose to pass it on to Werner Laurie, who printed it as *Laurie's Elementary Russian Grammar* 'for the business man'. It runs to 79 pages, in an edition some 4½ inches deep and 3½ inches wide.

It was, writes André, far and away the worst book he had ever turned out. At the same time it was the most successful, so far as sales went, though as he had given it away he did not benefit from this. For Werner Laurie sold the whole edition, at sevenpence a copy, to the British War Office, who issued it to every officer and man detailed for the expedition to Archangel.

In the meantime the author of the manual had decided, somewhat belatedly, to pay lip-service to discipline. When he got his proofs, he sent a set personally to the Ministre de la Guerre, head of the French equivalent of the War Office, with a request for permission to publish. The application went through the usual channels, and some months later André was officially notified that permission was refused. By this time the grammar had not only been printed, but was sanctioned by the British Army and was in the hands of every soldier destined for Russia.

André was unperturbed. There was no international crisis, not even a court-martial; the Archangel expedition petered out, and the course of the war was not noticeably affected.

During the two years that he spent with the 50th Division André appears to have enjoyed only one brief spell of home leave; this holiday led, in sad circumstances, to another publication, though the book in question was not written by himself. It was in September 1916 that he was able to spend three days with his wife and children at Wimbledon, but just before he got home his old friend A. S. Gardiner, whose encouragement had led to the writing of his first book, was knocked down by a bus in London and fatally injured. André's first act on arrival was to visit the dying man in Charing Cross Hospital, and Gardiner's last request to him was that he should arrange for the publication of a book he had written years before. He had been a keen cricketer, and the book was a collection of cricket stories and reminiscences called *The Old Crocks*. André saw it through the press in the following year, glad to be able to pay a literary debt that he felt he owed his old mentor. It is perhaps the only cricket book published under the auspices of a Frenchman.

Service in the fighting zone ended in June 1917, when André was transferred, still as interpreter, to the Canadian Forestry Corps at La Joux, in the Jura Mountains on the Swiss border. From then on, and for the rest of the war, life was easier. Shortly after the move he was appointed a member of the French Secretariat to the Allied Maritime Transport Council, dealing with the allocation of tonnage between France, Britain and the United States for movement of food, munitions and raw materials.

The Council met sometimes in Paris and sometimes in London; so André moved once again between the two cities in which he had spent most of his life. And he had plenty of time to enjoy the beloved company of his family.

In London the usual chairman of the Council was Winston Churchill, with whom André was greatly impressed. On one occasion Churchill interrupted an interpreter with a minor correction of a French word that his opposite number,

Monsieur Loucheur, had used. 'I knew then,' writes André, 'that Churchill's accent in French might be rather funny, but that his knowledge of French was truly remarkable.' It is not an attribute normally associated with that particular statesman.

Came the Armistice, and André expected to be released at once. But Monsieur Clemental, the French Ministre du Commerce, asked him to draft for him a clause for the Peace Treaty protecting French wine from German competition. André did so, producing a stipulation that the *appellations contrôlées* now imposed should be binding in Germany as they were in France. His suggestion was adopted, and so he had a share in the post-war settlement of Europe, appropriately championing the interests of French wine-growers.

It was a fitting end to his war service.

-5-

Days of Wine and Roses

FINALLY demobilised in January 1919, André returned without difficulty to the old routine. He had never lost touch with the champagne trade. In his forties now, he was a respected figure in the commercial life of London. Pommery were only too glad to have him back.

It was not all plain sailing, and André, experienced wine shipper though he was, met problems that taxed his expertise. War had exacted its toll. The old spirit of camaraderie in the trade had to some extent evaporated; commercial morality had, in his own words, 'suffered from years of wholesale destruction, looting and killing accepted as the "fortune of war", when it was not hailed as heroism'. The new spirit of cut-throat competition was not in accord with his temperament.

There were changes, also, in the quality of the product that it was his business to sell. In pre-war years only certain champagnes, wines of years of individuality, had been sold with the mark of a vintage. André in his early days with Pommery had concentrated on selling the 1900, 1904 and 1906; the rest was non-vintage champagne. Now, however, every year was shipped as a vintage by one or more of the champagne firms, and with the development of the technique of wine-making there was less discernible difference between the various brands and various years. Talking half a century later, André told his young friend Hugh Johnson how in the early 1900s he could look at diners at restaurant tables near his own and amuse himself by pronouncing on whether they were drinking an 1892 or an 1893 champagne. 'All '92s, whatever the brand, were pale straw and all the '93s were quite dark reddish gold. But I defy anyone today to tell a 1961 from a 1962, or for that matter from any other vintage. Why? Because champagne must now be light and colourless.' Standardisation, in fact, had become the order of the day.

André was not, where wine was concerned, an uncritical *laudator temporis acti*. He welcomed technological innovations, and was always ready to move with the times. Nevertheless he could not but regret the loss of character and individuality that some of these innovations entailed.

A more serious headache was concerned with the economics of the wine trade. Pommery were prospering more than ever in the post-war boom, but there were pitfalls ahead. Before 1914 rates of exchange were relatively stable, but now there were fluctuations. Champagne, a French product, was sold in England for sterling, but could be bought by anybody in France for francs, and the franc was liable to depreciation. This uncertainty was to lead in due course to the one great setback in André Simon's almost uniformly successful career. But this was in the future. All that seemed necessary in 1919 was watchfulness and good judgement.

There were changes too in André's private life, albeit of a minor nature. The family were growing up. Jeanne, the eldest child, was in her eighteenth year; the youngest, Madeleine, in her seventh. The two boys, André and Peter, were at Stonyhurst, under the direction of the Jesuits, whose teaching would be the dominating influence in the life of one of them.

The time would obviously come when some or all of the five would leave the shelter of the parental roof. In fact that time was not far ahead, but in the meantime it was the care of the father to give them the happiest possible home life. It so happened that the lease of the Wimbledon house was nearing its end. No. 8 The Downs was a big house with a garden, and André had become a keen gardener. He and Edith decided to move closer to central London, but both for their own sake and for that of the children they still wanted a garden. The answer was two homes.

First the Simons took a flat in Westminster, No. 6 Evelyn Mansions, Carlisle Place. It was convenient for André's main interests, close to Victoria Station from which he could get to the City by underground, and, equally important, could catch the boat train for his frequent visits to his native country. Green Park and St James's Park were close at hand. Moreover, a matter which weighed with the Simons, Evelyn Mansions is almost next door to Westminster Cathedral. For the next half-century the staunchly Catholic André, whenever he was in London, was to be seen almost daily at the 7 a.m. Mass in the cathedral.

Next came the purchase of a house in the country. The eventual choice was Little Hedgecourt, a property at Felbridge, near East Grinstead on the Sussex-Surrey border. It consisted of two adjoining cottages, one old but modernised, with twenty-eight acres of land which included an artificial lake.

In *By Request* André describes Little Hedgecourt as being as unsuitable a purchase as could possibly be. He was rather in the habit of commenting on his ventures in some such terms; in fact he and Edith soon converted their country home into a place of delight. They built a third cottage and employed two gardeners. They also built an open-air theatre; André always had an affection for the stage.

One of the first priorities, naturally enough, was the digging of a wine cellar. Next came the installation of a lawn tennis court and a bowling green. But most ambitious of all was the creation of a cricket ground.

André had developed an affection unusual in a Frenchman for the most English of games. It undoubtedly appealed to his aesthetic taste, and his interest in it had been aroused by A. S. Gardiner. The site for the Little Hedgecourt ground, in an eight-acre field bounded by conifers, was chosen, and the laying out of the pitch supervised, by no less a person than Percy Fender, most famous and dynamic of Surrey captains, who was a member of the wine trade and a close friend of Pommery's agent.

André soon became popular among his country neighbours, though in the nature of things he was not much at Felbridge except at weekends. He became the president of the local cricket club, a rare distinction indeed for a foreigner. Cricket in fact played a great part in the summer life of Little Hedgecourt, which itself put a team into the field to play Felbridge and the Lingfield Police eleven; André *fils* recruited the house side, bringing in his Stonyhurst friends as well as any neighbours he could find. The highlight, however, of those happy Augusts was the match known as Beer *versus* Wine. André has the following to say of this convivial annual fixture:

> The Wine side was a strong one and invariably won, not because of Fender, Tennyson, and other first-class cricketers who were then in the Wine Trade, not because of our umpires, Arthur Spencer, Alfred Heath, or O. T. Norris, but because wine and beer flowed freely for all who were thirsty, and the beer boys could not resist having their fill of wine, whilst the others were quite content with beer; I know, because I was O.C. Drinks on such occasions, and it was quite obvious to me that wine and first-class cricket are not the best of partners.

This final reflection is perhaps the nearest André ever came to a denunciation of wine. But it might equally well be interpreted as a criticism of cricket.

André and Edith were the best of hosts. The new cellar was always full, and there were innumerable parties at Little Hedgecourt to which it was a valued privilege to be invited. For the Simons' silver wedding in 1925 there were more than two hundred guests. The date was 17 October, but André's consistent good luck did not desert him. There was brilliant sunshine the whole day.

André might say what he liked about the unsuitability of the site he had chosen, but the many friends with whom he was always delighted to share its amenities were enchanted with the home he had created.

What he really thought of both Little Hedgecourt and 6 Evelyn Mansions is better indicated by the fact that through all the rest of his long life he never felt the need to make another move.

There was no halt in his literary activity; publications continued to pour almost incessantly from his pen. The Wine Trade Club was still flourishing, and André in 1919 produced two books for its education committee: *Food and Drink* and *Alcohol*. The same year saw a bigger venture. The publisher Gerald Duckworth, himself a noted wine-lover, had become a close friend and offered to publish whatever André chose to submit. André said he could not find the time to write a new book, but he agreed to resurrect some articles he had written before the war for a now defunct magazine, *Land and Water*, and work them up into a full-length publication. The result was *Wine and Spirits: The Connoisseur's Textbook*, duly published by Duckworth. It was, in the author's words, 'the first of my books to be "published" in a business manner, and offered for sale to the public by booksellers in London and the Provinces.' It was followed in the following year by *The Blood of the Grape: The wine trade text book*, in which the most recent lectures to the Wine Trade Club education committee were given similar treatment. This too was published by Duckworth.

There is indeed little sign that Pommery's agent was at this time too busy for literary composition. The flow of publication continued unchecked, though admittedly much of what he produced was revision of what he had written before. Yet in this same year of 1920 he brought out a book, in French, of quite a different nature from anything that had previously come from his pen.

In the early days of the war he had stood as godfather to the baby son, born in December 1914, of one of his soldier friends, Eugène Sivet. Now he published *Le Livre de mon Filleul*, which he described as '*lettres écrites pendant la guerre par un simple soldat à son filleul, le fils d'un de ses camarades de l'hiver 1914–1915*'. This inscription can hardly be taken literally. The form of the book, a series of essays of approximately equal length, precludes its being taken as reproductions of letters actually sent. Georges Sivet, moreover, was only five years old when the book appeared in print; he had hardly been of an age during the war to digest the precepts it contained. It is in fact a treatise of moral and spiritual guidance divided into nine sections entitled *La Vie*, *La Lutte*, *Les Armes*, *La Foi*, *L'Esperance*, *La Charité*, *Le Dogme*, *La Morale* and *Le Culte*, couched in simple French and reflecting André's happy philosophy and deep religious faith; its Catholic orthodoxy is vouched for by the fact that it carries the *Imprimatur* of the Bishop of Southwark, at that time the well-known Monsignor (later Archbishop) Peter Amigo. It was published by the Anglo-French Booksellers.

The book, which runs to 218 pages, shows that André did not regard godfatherhood as just a formality, to be forgotten once the christening was over. And young Georges was not the only child he had in mind. In his personal copy, preserved until recently at Little Hedgecourt, after the words

'*Le Livre de mon Filleul*' on the title page he added: '*et de ma fille Madeleine. A.L.S.*' Madeleine, who was a little older than Georges Sivet, was in due course to devote herself to the religious life. One wonders what part her father's book played in influencing her decision.

From the particular to the general. There followed, three years later, another book with a philanthropic purpose, likewise written in the author's native tongue. The French Benevolent Society was a London charity dedicated to the care of destitute French immigrants who for one reason or another were unable to return to their own country. It had been founded by Comte Alfred d'Orsay in 1842, at a time when some of the intended beneficiaries had been eking out a precarious existence since the French Revolution. The charity became associated with the wine trade through J. L. P. Lebègue, from Bordeaux, founder of the famous firm which bears his name, who was elected president in 1909. The 1914–1918 war brought an increase in the number of French refugees, and the work of the society correspondingly increased; Lebègue decided that the time had come to provide for the future. André Simon struck him as the ideal successor to himself and in 1919 he approached the younger man with the request that he would associate himself with the society and put himself forward as a candidate if and when the presidency became vacant.

André agreed, rather reluctantly because of his many commitments; what he did not expect was that he would be called on to assume office in a matter of weeks. But so it turned out. Lebègue died suddenly, after a fall from his horse in Hyde Park, and André was promptly elected president.

He threw himself into the new venture with his customary zeal. His first act, characteristically, was to give a dinner in aid of the Benevolent Society. It took place at the Connaught

Rooms, and the French Ambassador, Paul Cambon, presided. All the guests came by invitation, but each found a card in his place at the dinner asking him to name a sum to be given to the society. The amount raised, after all expenses had been paid, was just over £2,000, no mean sum in 1919.

This was a good beginning, and as the years passed the president continued to do all he could to further the aims of the French Benevolent Society. Naturally, being André, he wrote a book in its interests. Called *Les Pauvres de France en Angleterre*, and written in French because it was to French benevolence that he was appealing, it consisted of a number of moving sketches of the types of French down-and-out that the charity was endeavouring to help, the flotsam and jetsam of world war that found itself stranded in a foreign country.

Again being André, he persuaded a number of leading artists to illustrate his book with drawings. They included Bernard Partridge and Frank Brangwyn, as well as his own brother Jacques Simon. *Les Pauvres de France en Angleterre* was printed at the author's expense and the proceeds given to the French Benevolent Society.

The dozen years or so that followed the 1914–18 war were a time of singular felicity. The return of peace brought with it a taste for light-hearted enjoyment; the great depression ahead was no more thought of than the rise of Adolf Hitler. The Roaring Twenties, the age of Kate Meyrick and *Vile Bodies*, had other things in mind. André may have had little enough in common with the Bright Young People, or even with the young Evelyn Waugh; but more decorous pleasures were rife as well as theirs. Champagne was in demand in the boom, and André, with a free hand in the sale of Pommery, was able to expand the market and to feather his own nest comfortably and legitimately in doing so.

He and Percy Thellusson, retaining the Pommery agency, had formed themselves into a small private company, each holding fifty per cent of the shares. They bought no champagne except from Pommery of Rheims, and Pommery sold no champagne for re-sale in Britain except to them. The benefit was mutual. André was able to live his life to the full: a life of comfort, sociability and epicurean enjoyment.

He did quite a bit of travelling. Sometimes one or more of the Simon children would accompany him, as did his wife, on the trips abroad which he contrived to make at this time. The principal destination was South Africa. The land of gold and diamonds was a prime beneficiary of the boom, and the market there for champagne was virtually unlimited. Percy Thellusson could always be left in charge of the London agency for any reasonable period. Between 1919 and 1931 André paid some half-dozen visits to the Cape to boost the sales of Pommery. He took the opportunity to study and advise on South Africa's native wine, which had great natural potential but was not as yet being adequately developed.

Amid all this activity he managed to find the time for wide reading. From early years he had been a scholar and a historian; he never again wrote anything on the scale of *The History of the Wine Trade in England*, but he did, in 1926, turn out what was in fact a fourth volume of that work. Entitled *Bottlescrew Days*, it deals with wine drinking in England in the eighteenth century, and was published by Duckworth.

It was his historical research which made him a book collector on a formidable scale. In his early youth he spent what money he could spare from his then meagre income on the purchase of books, both English and French. They were mostly historical, and as time went on his interests became more specialised. When the Wine Trade Club was formed, and he became the chairman of its education committee, one of his main occupations, in addition to the delivery of lectures on wine in all its aspects, was the building up of a wine library on behalf of the club. In doing so he was fired with the collector's passion, and bought books for his own pleasure as well. Every rare book on wine that came into the market was seized upon, and in due course his own private wine library assumed proportions that have seldom if ever been surpassed.

The felicity of his private life was undisturbed, though half-way through the 1920s the dispersal of the Simon family, which he and Edith had always known to be inevitable, began. Jeanne, the oldest daughter, who was always her father's favourite, was the first to leave home. She was married in 1925 to William Rouyer Guillet, French-born but a naturalised Englishman, who with his elder brother ran a firm for the importation of brandy. Their father, Emile Guillet, was associated with André in the French Benevolent Society.

Two years later there was a second defection from the family circle. Peter, the younger son, had early in life felt the call of religion. On leaving Stonyhurst in 1927 he immediately joined the Society of Jesus, entering on his noviciate at Manresa House, the Jesuit college at Roehampton.

There was, naturally, an element of sadness in this departure of a son of whom, in the nature of things, his parents would catch only intermittent glimpses in the years to come. But André was the last person to oppose such a move. He had always encouraged his sons' religious development, and in 1925 had written, in French, a book of devotion for their particular benefit. Entitled *Nolite Timere*, it was published by Burns Oates and Washbourne.

He was in the habit of joining the Old Boys' Holy Week retreat at Stonyhurst. On one of these occasions he told Peter that, if his family responsibilities should ever cease, he would like to become a Jesuit lay brother and look after the Stonyhurst library; he would be quite ready to drink water daily and 'pop' on Sundays. Father Peter Simon has his doubts. 'He would soon have tired of a diet of Lancashire hot-pot and college cabbage.'

He conferred his parental benediction on his son's vocation when, soon after Peter had begun his noviciate, he visited him at Manresa. Touring the walled garden, he noted with approval that it contained a greenhouse with a flourishing shoot of the Hampton Court vine.

André's twin passions, wine and literature, led him to Ye Sette of Odd Volumes. This rather preciously named dining club, which André joined in 1931, had a membership mostly of lawyers and writers, and André owed his introduction to it to a much younger friend, a barrister named Maurice Healy, to whom he was devoted. Healy, soon to be a K.C., was the nephew of Tim Healy, the well-known Irish MP, whom André had known before the war through his old friend A. S. Gardiner, and it was the elder Healy who asked him to keep a kindly eye on his nephew when Maurice began to practise at the English bar.

Maurice Healy had grown up as a teetotaller, seeing around him in his childhood the horror of Irish poverty and the devastating effect of cheap liquor in those days of destitution. The guidance of a wise old priest, and later the experience of civilised drinking in officers' messes in his war service, taught him the error of his ways, and he was now learning all he could about wine. His chief tutor was André Simon, who in later years habitually referred to Maurice Healy as his 'very dear disciple'. Healy became, as well as an eminent figure at the English bar, a wine-lover and a writer on the subject comparable with his preceptor, renowned as much for his wit and urbanity as for his knowledge.

André's connection with Ye Sette of Odd Volumes is chiefly notable as having first brought him into contact with A. J. A. Symons, who was destined to play an important part in his career. Symons, principally remembered now as the author of *The Quest for Corvo*, the biography of that strange and tortured character Frederick Rolfe, self-styled Baron

Corvo, was a volatile, persuasive, enthusiastic bibliophile with a taste for good food and wine, whose unusual and scintillating personality attracted André to him even more than did their common interests.

Alphonse (he preferred to call himself 'Alroy') James Albert Symons had, so far as is known, no family connection with the Edith Symons who was now Madame André Simon. A minor curiosity is the frequency with which names closely resembling his own cropped up in André's life.

One club led to another. Symons had started, virtually on his own, the First Edition Club, described by André as 'a highly desirable institution, providing a place where bookish men could meet, dine and wine and chat pleasantly together, besides publishing limited small editions of fine books, holding exhibitions of books and documents likely to increase both the interest in and the knowledge of typography, calligraphy, bibliography and allied arts.'

Symons had recently incorporated his venture as a limited company. The First Edition Club Ltd was launched in a blaze of glory, being opened by King Manoel of Portugal, who had been living for many years in exile in England. It had excellent, ornate premises in Bedford Square, above which Symons and his wife entertained brilliantly and lavishly.

'A.J.', as he was generally known, had no difficulty in recruiting his new friend for his club. André in fact was enchanted with the whole idea and became an enthusiastic member. In January 1931 he gave for the club an exhibition of his own books and manuscripts, celebrated with a princely dinner mainly provided by himself. The guests enjoyed oysters, grilled fillets of beef, woodcock paté and a ripe Wensleydale, and the wines included a 1915 Pommery, Château Haut-Brion 1904 and Corton 1906; the brandy was an 1875 Hine.

What André did not know was that the company was

hopelessly unsound financially. Symons had no capital of his own. His persuasive eloquence had brought the financial support of influential and trusting friends, but his optimistic forecast of a membership of three thousand was unfulfilled. The figure was nearer three hundred.

It could not, and did not, last. By 1932 the First Edition Club Ltd had ceased to exist, though as a private club the institution went on in much more modest circumstances. The grand premises in Bedford Square were given up, and A.J. was compelled to dispose of his fine collection of books. He and his friends, including André, lost heavily, though such was the power of his personality that pity outweighed resentment. André, whose friendship with Symons was uninterrupted, does not tell us to what his own loss amounted. Whatever it was, he was soon to find that he could ill afford it. But this he did not foresee.

For the moment he took it all in his stride. He was still riding on the crest of the wave, a popular figure in London and accepted as a leader in his own line of country. He had friends in most walks of life. Looking through the files of his correspondence, preserved until recently at Little Hedgecourt, one finds the names of a fair cross-section of the eminent of the post-war period. Artists, writers, musicians, actors and actresses, sportsmen, provided only that they appreciated the good things of life, were glad to enjoy his company.

For André himself this was a source of satisfaction. He basked in friendship, and if his friends were men and women of distinction so much the better. Literature, it was to be expected, provided the most considerable number: Hilaire Belloc, Horace Annesley Vachell, Rebecca West, Hugh Walpole, Osbert Sitwell, Alec Waugh. In the world of art there were Bernard Partridge, James Gunn, Gerald Kelly; in music Mark Hambourg; in the theatre Gerald du Maurier, Alice Delysia, Sacha Guitry and Yvonne Printemps; in sport (or at any rate cricket) Percy Fender, Lionel Tennyson, C. M. Wells. The names also crop up of Mrs Winston Churchill, Lord Dawson of Penn, and Lord Methuen.

Belloc was a valued friend, and it seems curious that the list does not include his *alter ego*, Gilbert Keith Chesterton. G.K. was almost of an age with André; both their lives centred in literature and wine, and with their joviality, conviviality and capacity for friendship they were two of a kind. The letters, however, supply no indication of contact. Inquiry among members of the Simon family reveals that they did know each other but were never on intimate terms.

There was another towering figure in the worlds of literature and wine whom André apparently never encountered in the flesh, yet who was, albeit fortuitously, a major influence in his life. This was George Saintsbury.

Professor Saintsbury was a titan of academic letters. Born in 1845, during the last quarter of the nineteenth century and the early years of the twentieth he turned out a mass of writing which in sheer volume put that of André Simon to shame, dealing with virtually the whole corpus of English and French literature. His scholarship was profound, his views provocative. Rival scholars crossed swords with him at their peril.

With it all he was a *bon vivant* of the first order; his knowledge of wine was catholic and encyclopaedic. And in his old age he turned his pen to the subject of his second passion in life.

When, at the age of seventy, Saintsbury retired from the Regius Professorship of English Literature at Edinburgh University, he sold off the contents of his well-stocked cellar. It was a wrench, but he had his reasons – not only of economics but of health and of accommodation. But he still had the cellar-book in which he had lovingly recorded his purchases and his potations. The book which reached the public in 1920 was at least partly a work of nostalgia.

Notes on a Cellar-Book was quickly recognised as a classic of wine writing. It struck new ground. There had been wine books before, but in most cases they were technical treatises turned out for the wine trade. Here was a publication catering for the amateur devotee of the juice of the grape, the mellow reflections of an urbane scholar on the joy that good wine confers, enlivened with a wealth of quotations from the innumerable authors that Saintsbury knew so well, and of whom his favourites were Dryden and Thackeray.

The vintages described have mostly lost their relevance through the passage of time. But Saintsbury's book remains a delight to read.

It may be assumed that André read *Notes on a Cellar-Book* as soon as it came out. At any rate he came to regard Saintsbury as one of his prime mentors in the study of wine. The book undoubtedly influenced his own writing; many years later he followed its plan closely in one of his minor works, *Notes on the Late J. Pierpont Morgan's Cellar Book*.

What was more important was that the book led to the formation of yet another dining club; one that, gastronomically, was of higher distinction than any that had yet been launched.

The genesis of the Saintsbury Club was at No. 24 Mark Lane. The progenitors were André Simon, Maurice Healy, A. J. A. Symons, J. C. Squire and Guy Knowles.

All five were literary men as well as wine-lovers, and when, on 5 February 1931, eleven years after the publication of *Notes on a Cellar-Book*, they were lunching together and enjoying a perfect bottle of Château Haut-Brion 1874, the talk turned to George Saintsbury. Jack Squire said it was a pity the great apostle of wine could not be with them to enjoy this marvellous vintage, and he went on to lament that the illustrious professor should be living almost sightless at Bath, friendless and all but forgotten.

Under the influence of pre-phylloxera claret the idea

quickly took shape. Before the five friends parted it had been resolved that they should invite the professor to a dinner to be held in his honour. There was some discussion on the date; Saintsbury's eighty-sixth birthday was not till October, so it was decided to make it his name-day, the Feast of St George, on 23 April.

Generosity was poorly rewarded. Saintsbury was indeed living a solitary life at Bath; but it seems that he preferred it that way. Always an individualist, he had become a somewhat cantankerous old gentleman, who wanted only to be left alone. The cordial invitation sent by Jack Squire on behalf of himself and his friends was turned down brusquely and without thanks.

This would have been enough for most admirers, however convivial their intention. Not so for the light-hearted five. Another missive was sent to the professor, to the effect that they were ready to go to Bath on St George's Day in the hope of entertaining him to lunch or dinner at his choice. Saintsbury's reply has not been preserved, but we have André's summary of what it contained. It was almost indecipherable, but André grasped its import. This was that Saintsbury had no intention of lunching or dining with his would-be hosts on any date, at any place or in any circumstances.

Even now André and his friends were not deterred. Their proceedings were a triumph of wine over manners. They had resolved to honour Professor Saintsbury, and honour him they would, whatever might be his own feelings in the matter. They were determined to go ahead with a dinner, though not on St George's Day. It was held at the Connaught Rooms on 28 May, with D. S. MacColl, a wine comrade of André, in the chair. MacColl gave a eulogy of the very much absent guest of honour, after which André proposed the toast of Wine. Then Maurice Healy rose with a practical proposal. Why, he asked, should those present not form themselves into a dining club, to meet twice a year, on or about St

George's Day and on or about the professor's birthday, 23 October? 'Those two dinners would be occasions for discussing the merits of new books and new vintages incidentally, but primarily for keeping alive the memory of George Saintsbury.'

The suggestion was received with the enthusiasm that had marked the whole episode. A telegram was sent to Saintsbury inviting him to be president of the club; it was characteristically unacknowledged, but he was elected none the less. More than this, it was decided that he should be president not for life but 'in perpetuity'. André became cellarer, Squire editor, and Symons secretary. Other members of the committee were Healy and André's old friend Ian Campbell.

André loved a good story, and it is fair to emphasise that his account of how the Saintsbury Club came into being has not been universally credited. Some who knew the professor have averred that he would never have been so churlish. It is notable that Maurice Healy, who also recorded the events, makes no mention of a flat refusal to attend any celebration. It may be that the truth is to be found simply in the illegibility of the Saintsbury calligraphy.

The inaugural dinner was held on the agreed date, 23 October 1931, at Vintners' Hall. It was a great occasion, and a gastronomic joy. The menu and list of wines are worth giving in full:

Consommé Excelsior	Sercial da Donna Isabel Esmeralda
Blanchailles Diablées	Montrachet Bâtard 1926
Filet Mignons Florentine	Pontet Canet 1920
Perdreaux Rôtis à la Broche Salade Parisienne	Château Latour 1878
Champignons au Gratin	

Pommes D'Allington   Quarles Harris 1851
Noix à la Glacé

Café   Hine's 1844

The madeira, presented by Stephen Gaselee, was a centenarian. The Château Latour, an imperial (equal to eight bottles) was the gift of Ian Campbell, and the Bâtart-Montrachet that of André Simon. J. C. Squire was the chairman, but the evening belonged above all to Hilaire Belloc.

Belloc had been chosen to propose the toast of Professor Saintsbury. When the moment came he rose uncertainly, swayed, and uttered three words: 'I am drunk.' There was an embarrassed silence. Then he hummed, coughed, and proceeded to make a scintillating speech, covering the whole range of good and bad writing and of good and bad wine. When he sat down there was appreciative acclamation, and next day André asked him to put the essence of his speech down on paper for the benefit of the club. He replied that he could not remember a single word of what he had said.

At the second dinner of the Saintsbury Club, on 21 April 1932, again at Vintners' Hall, Belloc was in the chair, doubtless as reward for his performance at the first. At the third, in October of the same year, the honour fell to André. The highlight of this meal was another imperial of Château Latour 1878.

When the time came for the next, Saintsbury was no more; he died at Bath on 28 January 1933, aged eighty-seven. He was, André tells us, ungracious to the last. When a club delegation went to Bath with a wreath, it was only to be told that he had been buried at Southampton.

But the club dedicated to his memory still survives. It still dines twice a year on the best of good food and good wine. And its president, half a century after his death, is still Professor George Saintsbury.

–6–

The Good Life

IT was in these carefree days of the 1920s that André Simon developed the philosophy that gave him his sense of purpose in life. His ideas on wine, and on the part that wine played in the enhancement of the benefits of civilisation, had of course been taking shape at least since his earliest connection with Pommery; but it is reasonable to assume that it was not till the post-war years that they took the form of mature reflections leading to a way of perfection.

The humanist princes of the Renaissance had pursued what came to be known as the Good Life. Taking all knowledge as their province, they steeped themselves in all that could at that time be found of the literature of the world, but with particular concentration on the classical sages of Greece and Rome. Equal attention was paid to the pictorial arts, which in Italy at least were the glory of the period. Music too played its part, as did the material luxuries and pleasures of the mundane world.

André, cultured bibliophile and enlightened man of the world that he was, was fully in accord with the Renaissance ideal. He too pursued the Good Life. But he differed in emphasis from the humanists. With them gastronomy took a comparatively minor place. This was natural. They had no knowledge of vintage wines, the art of maturing which had been lost since Roman times; and the pleasures of the table were, by the standards of later ages, gross. To André, on the other hand, gastronomy was all-important: not because he regarded it as being of a higher nature than the cultivation of intellectual advance or of the liberal arts, but because it was at the centre of his own existence and he could make it the core of an all-embracing civilised equilibrium. His concept of the Good Life was therefore founded on the proper appreciation of wine and food.

He defined gastronomy as 'the intelligent choice and appreciation of whatever is best in food and drink for Gaster the belly, as well as a lively sensual satisfaction to our sense and sight, smell and taste'. A gastronome, he held, must 'be born with a good sense of smell and taste, gifts that no money can buy'. But given those gifts of God anybody could achieve that harmony of civilised enjoyment that made gastronomy an essential part of the pattern of good living. Moderation was as important as the cultivation of taste. 'Gastronomy stands or falls by moderation. No gourmand and no glutton can be a gastronome. No hard drinker can be a gastronome. His taste-buds get blurred and seared by alcohol.' At the same time, if a man was endowed by nature with a big appetite or a large ability to absorb liquor, there was no reason why he should not gratify either or both, so long as he did not exceed his natural capacity, and what he ate and drank was of good quality. André himself was in fact a prime example of this proviso. Blessed with good health and a magnificent constitution, he was able throughout his life to consume quantities of food and draughts of liquor that to most people would qualify for a stronger term than excess; but he never strained his capacity beyond its natural limit. And what he ate and drank, provided the choice was his own, was always of the best.

Quality, in his view, was of the first importance. There was no excuse, except perhaps politeness, for eating inferior food or drinking bad wine. Expense was a consideration he was apt to brush aside. The best need not mean the dearest. People, he would say, who insisted that they could not afford to eat and drink well would think nothing of spending twice as much on a taxi fare as they would on a bottle of wine. Exaggerated parsimony in the matter of taxis was, as a matter of fact, one of André's endearing characteristics. Even in old age he was known to stand in pouring rain waiting for a bus rather than indulge in the extravagance of taking a taxi that he could very easily afford.

Eating and drinking well constituted one of the main elements of civilised existence, harmonising with the other essentials of the Good Life. In *In the Twilight* he devoted a passage to one of his colleagues in the Saintsbury Club, whom he described as the model and pattern of a gastronome of his children's generation. 'He was the most generous host with always a gracious welcome for all, which is rather uncommon among such wealthy people as he was. His taste was exquisite and catholic. It was not only his food and wine that were of the best, but his pictures, glassware, silver and furniture. Everything he lived with had beauty and harmony.' This was the ideal at which André aimed.

At the end of the decade he embodied his views in *The Art of Good Living*. This book, described on the title page as 'A Contribution to the better Understanding of Food and Drink together with a Gastronomic Vocabulary and a Wine Dictionary', was published by Constable in 1929. The original edition carried a foreword by Maurice Healy, who had become the most zealous of André's followers.

The Art of Good Living, which opens with an introduction proclaiming the philosophy the author had now developed, but incidentally giving an interesting account of the history of London hotels and restaurants, is a practical guide to the pleasures of the table, designed to illustrate the harmony that should exist between food and wine, and to show in detail exactly which beverages accord best with the dishes a cultured Englishman is accustomed to enjoy.

This was the first book in which André dealt in detail with food. Always he had been a wine specialist, and he still gave wine priority; but in *The Art of Good Living* he allotted as much space to the solid part of a meal as to the liquid. It is in no sense a cookery book. Actually, though he would come to be accepted as almost as great an authority on food as on wine, it is recorded that André never learned to cook. He preferred that others should do the work at the oven; his own rôle was that of guide, philosopher and friend.

His book, however, gives a multitude of useful guidelines on the good things that appear on plates, together with expositions of his own likes and dislikes. After an appreciative dissertation on chicken he writes: 'Ducks do not supply so happy a background as chickens do for the culinary artist to show off the picture which his imagination and science can produce for our palate to enjoy. They carry less meat upon their bones, and that possesses a stronger flavour, one which does not blend with many other flavours, and also one which soon palls upon the palate. To enjoy duck one must not have duck too often.' He goes on to say: 'Turkey, Goose, Guinea Fowl and Pigeon are really no better than Cygnets and Peacocks, once upon a time counted among the greatest delicacies. One should be content to meet them occasionally at some friend's dinner table without troubling to order them when one is the host.'

Reading his remarks on these birds so beloved of past ages, I cannot resist a personal reminiscence. Being interested in medieval dishes, and knowing that there was hardly anything in the food line that André had not eaten at some time or other, I once asked him if he had ever tasted swan. The answer, of course, was yes. What was it like, I pursued. He replied in one word, emphasised with even more than his usual rolling of r's: 'Fr-r-r-r-ightful.'

On the grouse André writes in *The Art of Good Living*:

'There is no finer bird in the world, gastronomically speaking, than a young Grouse during the last week in August or the first week in September, just plain roasted and with no other sauce than its own gravy. A red Graves, Haut Brion for choice, or a Graves of St. Emilion, such as Château Cheval Blanc, is most enjoyable with a young roast grouse at a time of the year when Burgundy may be found a little too heating.' But on the pig: 'Cold pickled pork or a grilled pork chop and onions are very good upon a cold day with a large draught of ale, but they are not mentioned at gastronomic reunions. As a matter of fact, the only part of the pig which is introduced into polite gastronomic society is the Ham.' He adds: 'With ham Champagne is best.'

When one turns to the wine sections of the book, the first thing that strikes one is the predominance of claret. This preference reflects the development of André's taste. Champagne was the first wine he studied, and to the end he retained his delight in its joy-giving qualities. But as time went on the more sophisticated virtues of the red wines of Bordeaux captivated his palate as they have those of countless wine-lovers through the generations. 'What other wine', we read in *The Art of Good Living*, 'is acceptable, and not only acceptable but enjoyable whether it be five or sixty years old, except Claret? There is no other. Where can anyone hope to find not a dozen, but a hundred wines, of any one vintage, all distinctive; of similar character yet different; all having a strong family likeness yet with a personality unmistakably their own? Nowhere except at Bordeaux . . . Why is it? It is because Claret possesses to a greater degree than any other wine the gift of individuality.'

In discussing André Simon's predilection for what to so many of us is the most blessed gift that even the juice of the grape has to offer, a brief dissertation on the history of claret is unavoidable.

Claret, the most natural of wines, in which human interference with the fermentation of grape juice is reduced to the minimum, was made in what is now the south-west of France, Gaul as it was then, at least as far back as the Roman conquest. In the twelfth century, through the accession to the English throne of Count Henry of Anjou (Henry II), who was married to Eleanor the heiress to the duchy of Aquitaine, the area known as Gascony, which was part of the duchy, became subject to the English crown. From then on, and throughout the remainder of the middle ages, the wine of Bordeaux, the Gascon wine, was regarded as almost an English product. Both red and white constituted the staple beverage in England's wine-drinking days, but red predominated. It was known as *clairet*, the wine of light, bright colour, and as made then was probably of a lighter tincture than the full red wine of today.

It was a simple wine and was drunk young. The Romans, with their *amphorae*, had known the secret of preserving wine so that it would age while keeping and improve its quality, but this secret did not survive the fall of the western Roman Empire. It was not till the end of the seventeenth century that the development of the bottle and of the cork, which had enabled Dom Pérignon to perfect the production of champagne, led to similar progress in the making of the red wines of Bordeaux and Burgundy. Even so, it was another century before great vintage clarets were developed. It was in the 'Comet Year' of 1811 that a vintage of singular splendour ushered in the era of glorious wines whose magnificence increased as they aged.

The next landmark in the history of claret was the official classification of 1855, initiated by Bordeaux brokers in preparation for a Paris international exhibition. Bordeaux's red wines, grown on estates usually known loosely as châteaux, are grouped in a number of regions of which four predominate – the Médoc, Graves, St Emilion and Pomerol. All produce fine wines, but when it was decided to classify the châteaux in something approaching an order of merit only the wines of the Médoc, by far the largest region, were surveyed.

Sixty châteaux, considered the best, figured in the 1855 classification. They were placed in five classes. Three alone attained the highest honour – the *premiers crus*, or 'first growths'; there were fifteen châteaux in the second class, fourteen in the third, ten in the fourth, and eighteen in the fifth.

The first growths were Château Lafite, Château Latour and Château Margaux; but classed alongside these three aristocrats was the greatest of the Graves wines, Château Haut-Brion, the only wine from outside the Médoc to be taken into consideration.

The classification has stood the test of time. Those four wines are still accepted as supreme among clarets, though officially associated with them now is Château Mouton-Rothschild, classed in 1855 as the first of the second growths.

There has never been any doubt among wine-lovers that claret and burgundy stand alone as the world's greatest red wines. As Saintsbury put it, claret is the queen of natural wines, the more robust burgundy the king. Nevertheless the 1855 classification set the seal on claret's regality. The entirely different system of production in Burgundy, with its small holdings and the division of individual vineyards among proprietors, does not lend itself to an order of merit of this nature.

It was a milestone in the history of claret, and there was nothing to show that disaster was ahead. In the meantime the score or so of years that followed the classification were marked by a series of magnificent vintages that were probably of higher quality than any other in the wine's history. The great clarets of 1858, 1864, 1865, 1870, 1871, 1875 and

1878 are only a memory now, but a host of eminent judges of wine have borne testimony to their splendour.

The blow, when it fell, was devastating. In the 1870s an experimenting French wine-grower imported some vines from America to see how they would do on French soil. As Alexis Lichine says in his authoritative book *Wines of France*, 'they did well, completely destroying nearly every vineyard in France.' For they brought with them, embedded in their roots, a burrowing louse, the phylloxera, endowed with quite extraordinary destructive power. Curiously enough, the American vines themselves had developed an immunity from the ravages of this pestiferous insect, the worst enemy wine has ever had; this was why the trouble was not detected in the first place. No such immunity applied to the French vines, which quickly became infected. The canker spread with astonishing rapidity, and vineyards were destroyed wholesale.

For a time it seemed that the entire European wine industry was ruined; the phylloxera soon made its presence felt beyond the frontiers of France, even reaching Madeira. Remedy after remedy was tried without avail. Then, in the early 1880s, the solution was found; scientists discovered and investigated the immunity of the American vines, and the New World, from which the plague had come, was called in to redress the balance of the Old. Uninfected American roots were imported in quantity, and French vines were grafted on to them. Within a few years the scourge was halted, and wine production was restored to something like its previous volume. Since then the advance in scientific technique has kept phylloxera at bay.

Claret was far from being the only victim of what Herbert Warner Allen, author of *A History of Wine*, aptly called 'an Attila from the New World, the Scourge of the Wine God'; the whole production of wine in the western world was affected. But the Bordeaux vineyards seem to have suffered most; the delicate nature of their red wines made them peculiarly vulnerable. After 1878, the last of the great pre-phylloxera vintages, it was many years before growths of anything like comparable quality were produced.

When, towards the end of the century, such wines did at last begin to appear, with the assistance of American vines, they took on the qualities of the old clarets – but with one important qualification. Wine-lovers have argued incessantly among themselves as to the respective merits of the pre-phylloxera and post-phylloxera clarets; but there is general agreement that the new wines have not the staying power of the old. Maurice Healy drank a Château Lafite of the Comet Year in 1926, when it was 115 years old, and recorded that it had 'not more than a suspicion of fading'. Warner Allen gave similar praise to a magnum of Château La Lagune 1858 drunk in the year of its centenary. It is said that anybody lucky enough to chance on a pre-phylloxera claret today may well find that it still preserves its supremacy. No such claim is likely to be made for anything produced since 1878.

In the late 1920s the great pre-phylloxera clarets had reached their half-century at least. Obviously they were becoming rare; but there were still a surprising number of bottles, magnums and occasionally larger vessels available for those who had the taste, the discrimination and the means to acquire them.

Prominent among such connoisseurs was André Simon, who at this period enjoyed a succession of glorious meals at which the finest clarets ever drunk were the most notable feature. One is able to share vicariously his indulgence in these illustrious wines through a book published in 1933. It is the practical counterpart to the theoretical treatise he had turned out in *The Art of Good Living*.

In his earlier days, when writing about meals and wines he

had enjoyed, André had trusted largely to his excellent gastronomic memory. But towards 1930 he acquired the habit of making immediate notes on what he had eaten and drunk and what he thought about the food and wine. So when it was suggested that he should write a book containing records of memorable meals he had the materials to hand.

The suggestion actually came from one of his wine-loving friends, the novelist Michael Sadleir, who had enjoyed his hospitality at many such meals. The title, *Tables of Content: Leaves from my Diary*, was Maurice Healy's idea, but it was Sadleir who devised the distinctive wrapper. This showed André and two of his oldest friends, Ian Campbell and Francis Berry, sitting over a magnum of claret at the Trocadero restaurant: three consummate connoisseurs in a pose of civilised contentment. I am assured by Anthony Berry, Francis's son, that the wine was Château Haut-Brion 1905.

A story attaches to this picture. One is struck by the fact that, although one or two figures are dimly discernible in the distant background, most of the tables are empty. It so happened that not long before, when a certain film star was dining at the Trocadero, a press photographer had taken a picture, which was duly published. Unfortunately, at another table, a lady was enjoying a tête-a-tête dinner with her lover, and her husband saw the photograph. Shortly afterwards he brought an action for divorce, at which the photograph was produced. Not only that, but the co-respondent sued the restaurant for damages. Now the Trocadero manager was taking no chances. He insisted on André and his friends waiting until customers at neighbouring tables had gone before any photographer was let loose.

André wrote in *By Request* that *Tables of Content*, which like its predecessor was published by Constable, was 'not the kind of book that had any chance of appealing to the great

British public'. Possibly not, at any rate at that time; yet it must rank as one of the most gratifying in all his literary output. It consists of more than a hundred menus of splendid dinners and luncheons, enjoyed in the best of good company and enriched by the ripe comments of a cultured and benevolent *bon vivant*. To a lover of wine and food there is nothing monotonous about the book. It breathes on every page the spirit of good living and good fellowship.

Many of the meals took place in the Pommery office at 24 Mark Lane, where André entertained his friends to lunches at which the best procurable wines were served. Guests at these included, of course, such old cronies as Francis Berry, Ian Campbell, Warner Allen, Maurice Healy and A. J. A. Symons; but the names also occur, at various times, of Stephen Gaselee, Gilbert Miller, Morton Shand, C. B. Cochran, J. C. Squire, C. M. Wells, Percy Fender, Walter Elliot, Max Pemberton, Drogo Montagu, Victor Rothschild: a fair cross-section of the most distinguished figures of the pre-1939 era. Most of these, and others of similar eminence, were at different times André's hosts in their own houses or at hotels or restaurants.

Tables of Content opens with a dinner given by Francis Berry at his house on Wimbledon Hill on 7 November 1928. His guests were given turtle soup, red mullet with *sauce bordelaise*, saddle of mutton and *foie gras de Strasbourg*, and the wines included Château Margaux 1900 and a magnum of Château Mouton-Rothschild 1869. Those present besides André, his host, and Berry's son George, were 'Sir Ernest Rutherford, Frank Taylor, Victory Seyd, A. J. B. Norris, all men "steeped" in wine, and Maurice Healy, the most willing pupil any of us professionals in the science of wine could wish to have.'

André was highly appreciative of the two clarets. The Mouton was 'a perfect specimen' of the 1869 vintage: 'Splendid colour, fair body and bouquet but finished dry.' But the best wine was the youngest, the Margaux 1900. It had 'absolutely no blemish: colour warm and brilliant; bouquet most attractive; body fleshy and silky; farewell sweet and discreet'. So in *Tables of Content*. In the original notebook on which the book was founded André had added: 'The finest Claret I have enjoyed for some time.' It was, in fact, one up for post-phylloxera.

This dinner set the pattern for many more repasts of a similar nature. Sometimes the food was simple, sometimes elaborate. Always it was of the best quality; always accompanied by the finest wines of classic vintages.

Every variety of wine was sampled at one time or other. There were a good number of burgundy dinners; a notable one took place at Sir Stephen Gaselee's house in Kensington in January 1929. One of those present was the Rumanian Minister Titulesco, a well-known figure in London and in international society at that time. Gaselee's guests drank that pre-eminent burgundy Clos de Vougeot, vintages 1889 and 1893, followed by an 1821 madeira. André was interested to note that the 1889 had lasted better than the younger wine. The 1893 'had retained a certain amount of vitality but there was neither fat nor flesh left on the great bony frame of what must have been once upon a time a very fine fellow. I called it a skeleton of a wine; Titulesco called it a ghost; Gaselee was nearer the mark, calling it a skeleton with the soul still in possession. A stricken giant, still breathing.'

At a luncheon at the Connaught Rooms later in the same year the object was to try out wines produced in different parts of the world from the same grape, the Pinot, which is associated mainly with burgundy and champagne. A distinguished company included Gerald du Maurier, Compton Mackenzie and Michael Sadleir, as well as those faithful stalwarts Maurice Healy, J. C. Squire and A. J. A. Symons. The wines included the little-known still red champagne which goes by the pleasant-sounding name of Bouzy; André

ANDRÉ SIMON

pronounced it delightful, but 'it was not understood by the majority of the men present who had never tasted it before'.

The majority, however, of these gastronomic celebrations were claret dinners or luncheons, and at an astonishing number of them the principal wine drunk was pre-phylloxera. Every now and then there would crop up the supreme Château Lafite 1864, the wine of which Warner Allen wrote in his *History of Wine*: 'I am still convinced that if there is a Platonic idea of Claret stored up in heaven, it is indistinguishable from Lafite 1864 in its greatest days.'

It had not always stayed the course. That consummate host Francis Berry gave a dinner in November 1930 at which it was preceded by Château Margaux 1900 and Château Haut-Brion 1899. 'The 1864 was too old. Francis would go down and open another bottle, and it was ever so much better than the first; most enjoyable, although it did not rob the 1900 of the first place tonight.' At a dinner at the Trocadero in the following month André had both a Lafite and a Latour of 1864; 'the Lafite was a little more worn, although by no means worn out.' But in the following April, when his host was Guy Knowles, 'the Lafite 1864 was absolutely wonderful; sound, soft and sweet. A magnificent sight: like one of the old sailing ships, its canvas all out in the blazing sun and ploughing the blue sea with ease and assurance, proud of its long past, unconcerned at the speed of smoky steamers and throbbing motor-boats. Grace and strength. Perfect harmony. Full marks.'

And so the catalogue of great wines goes on. Quotations could be multiplied. That André sometimes overdid the purple passages could hardly be denied. But he was dealing with imperial purple.

A curiosity of these memoirs of happy meals is that the presence of ladies is seldom mentioned. André was all his life fond of feminine company, and the wives of his hosts and guests must on a good many occasions have been present; yet not often do their names appear. Some of the parties, moreover, were at Evelyn Mansions, and some at Little Hedgecourt, where Edith Simon surely entertained her guests. Yet we find few allusions to her.

The solution must presumably be that even as late as 1930 the female half of humanity were not generally considered qualified to pronounce on good wine. And if they had nothing to contribute to the main aspect of gastronomic enjoyment there was no need to mention them. It seems strange, since elsewhere André pays generous tribute to the discrimination of his wife's palate. But it is otherwise difficult to account for the omission.

One exception refers to an unexpected visit to Little Hedgecourt by that great man of the theatre Charles B. Cochran and his wife in July 1931. 'C.B. rang up at 12, from London, to know if we were at the Cottage, and I told him that we were alone, my wife and myself; an almost unheard of thing for us to be without any children or friends on a Sunday at the Cottage. So they both motored down and shared with us the Sunday roast beef of Old England.'

André did them well. Champagne led the way – 'straight from the cellar, not iced; cool and crisp and an excellent prologue on a sunny Sunday morning.' And then:

The *1904 Haut-Brion* was surprisingly good: its bouquet most attractive; its colour beautiful; its body firm, full and silky; its good-bye a little dry, but pleasantly so. A delightful glass of Claret. It went well with the underdone sirloin, so well that we had nothing to drink with the freshly gathered garden peas, which were so sweet, in spite of the lettuce and small onions à la française, that I really did not know what would be the right wine to bring forth. A Claret would have tasted too dry and a Sauternes too sweet. Then I remembered that I had a bottle of Pommery 1889, which

Percy Fender had given me, and I thought that it might be just the thing. And indeed it was. It looked none too hopeful, being ullaged to below the shoulder, but the cork went off with a pop, and there was still plenty of life in the old boy . . .

This was an occasion which André remembered with particular pleasure. 'A perfectly simple, simply perfect and wholly unexpected Sunday lunch.'

A more notable exception to the general rule of ignoring the female sex was likewise connected with the theatre, and indirectly with Charles Cochran. Alice Delysia, most charming, cultivated and sophisticated of French actresses, might be described as the feminine counterpart of André Simon, and it is not surprising that they were friends. Delysia had been brought to London by Cochran, and in March 1929 she had the privilege of an invitation to a luncheon at the Mark Lane office, where she was given four 1915 burgundies – La Romanée, Corton, Nuits St Georges and Clos de Vougeot. 'Delysia loved them all. But then she has a very big heart. And she has a splendid head too. I know of no other woman who can enjoy her full share of good wine as she does. Bless her!' In the notebook André's tribute was a bit more explicit: 'She is the only woman I know who can drink a whole bottle of Burgundy – and a bit over – and enjoy every drop of it without being in the least tired!'

Nearly four years later, in January 1933, Delysia was again in London to appear in *Mother of Pearl* at the Gaiety, and on the first night she and her husband, George Denis, invited André to supper at the Savoy. He does not tell us whether Edith was also present. The main dishes were '*La Poularde en gelée "Mother of Pearl"*' and '*La Pêche Delysia et la Mousse aux fraises*', with a 1924 Château Haut-Brion and a 1920 Krug. Delysia 'had the most rousing reception. But what makes this supper worth recording is the true artist's touch, the glass of young, full-bodied red wine after the very hot and cheese-sprinkled *soupe à l'oignon*. It filled the bill as no Champagne nor any other wine could have done. Few people whom I know would have thought of it; fewer still, had they thought of it, would ever have had the courage to order Haut-Brion for supper at the Savoy, and yet it was the right thing without a doubt. Delysia is a great artist. Bless her!'

A supper such as this, in such delightful company, must have been a consolation to André at a most difficult time. Shortly before it took place the one outstanding setback in his almost uniformly successful career had occurred.

Fresh Woods

THE blow fell on 30 November 1932. On that day André, after more than thirty years' service with Pommery et Greno, was abruptly dismissed and deprived of all connection with the firm.

Details of the full circumstances have never been publicly stated, and to some extent these still remain obscure. André himself, partly at least out of regard for the feelings of his own family, was always reticent about the affair, which aroused great resentment in the champagne trade and some bitterness among the Simons themselves.

As to how the shock was administered, the accounts in *By Request* and *In the Twilight* differ slightly from each other. It seems best to accept the version recorded in the notebook from which the meals described in *Tables of Content* was taken; this at least was written down soon after the event took place, and probably on the same day.

The thirtieth of November is the Feast of St Andrew, which André was accustomed to celebrate as his name day. On this occasion he had planned one of his splendid luncheons at 24 Mark Lane; the guests were his old friends Ian Campbell, Francis Berry and Guy Knowles, together with Grant Richards the well-known author and publisher, and Richards's son-in-law John Taylour. The fare was simple, an omelette followed by fillet of beef and Cheddar cheese; but the wines, all clarets, were of the usual distinction – Château Léoville-Poyferré 1905, Château Pichon-Longueville 1895,

THE NINETY-SECOND MEETING OF

THE WINE AND FOOD SOCIETY

HELD AT THE CONNAUGHT ROOMS
GREAT QUEEN STREET, LONDON

on Thursday 24th May 1945 at One o'clock after noon

The Right Honourable S. M. Bruce
High Commissioner for Australia
in the Chair

supported by

The Right Honourable Vincent Massey
High Commissioner for Canada

The Right Honourable W. J. Jordan
High Commissioner for New Zealand

The Right Honourable Heaton Nicholls
High Commissioner for The Union of South Africa

THE FARE

Les Hors-d'Œuvre Jardinière
Le Pâté d'Oiselets Maison
L'Emincé de Champignons
La Salade de Saison
L'Entremets sucré Pompette
Le Café

THE WINES

White, Amber and Golden Wines from South Africa and Australia
Essays Fine Old S.A. Brandy

MEMBER'S NAME

TABLE

The 92nd meeting of the Wine and Food Society –
Victory Dinner menu, 24 May 1945

André Simon with Joy Fontes, now a Vice-President of the International Wine and Food Society, at a Chevaliers du Tastevin reunion in London

André Simon at the tomb of Dom Pierre Pérignon

André Simon, portrait by James Gunn

The cover of the menu to celebrate
the Diamond Wedding of André Simon and his wife

In the vineyards of 'Twee Jonge Gezellen'
with Mr N C Krone, 24 February 1965

'In merry mood'

At the Diamond Wedding party

Château Haut-Brion 1899, and Château Lafite 1878. An 1844 Hine's brandy was to end the meal.

It took place as arranged. But before setting down his comments, which were reproduced in the accustomed form in *Tables of Content*, the host wrote a preliminary passage in the notebook:

> As an apéritif, I was informed at noon by Albert Guillet and the Marquis de Polignac that the latter had offered 'his' agency to the two brothers Guillet, who had accepted same and would not require my services. On asking when I was expected to be out of Mark Lane, I was told that so long as I had removed my belongings and myself by the 1st of January 1933 all would be well. I advised Albert to go home and think it over again.
>
> In spite of this somewhat disturbing anti-cyclone I enjoyed the lunch very much. There was the comforting feeling of having friends whom one could trust and with whom to share boons and trials; there was, of course, no question of trials during lunch.

'I am sure,' he added at the end of his notes, 'that my five friends enjoyed this the last feast of Claret I shall ever preside over at Mark Lane; none of them, of course, suspected that less than an hour before lunch I had been given 30 days notice to quit after 30 years of office.'

Albert Guillet was the elder of the two brothers, brandy shippers, the younger of whom was married to André's daughter Jeanne. Presumably he did 'go home and think it over again', for rather belatedly a suggestion came that André should stay on as a figurehead, with no control over the agency. But this his pride would not allow him to accept.

As to the cause of this sudden change of front on the part of Pommery, André in his autobiographical works blames it all on the financial crisis that burst on Britain in 1931. Pommery and Greno Ltd, the private company in which he and Percy Thellusson held fifty per cent each of the shares, worked on the arrangement that it bought no champagne except from Pommery of Rheims, who in return sold none for re-sale in Britain and the British Empire except to the London company who were its agents. Pommery and Greno Ltd bought in francs and sold in sterling, and when, in September 1931, Britain went off the gold standard, and the value of the pound promptly fell from 124 francs to 80, the company found that it could not meet the debts that ensued.

André himself did not think the situation desperate. He was confident that the company would weather the storm; only time was needed. Thellusson disagreed. He considered that the champagne trade was ruined, and the only solution was for the company to go into voluntary liquidation; then there would be enough money to pay off everybody in full, Rheims alone excepted. André would not hear of what he regarded as a panic surrender to fortune, and the upshot was that he agreed to buy Thellusson's shares at their face value, and then, as Percy put it, 'I could be as quixotic as I pleased and lose all my money – but not his.'

So it was that André Simon became the sole agent of Pommery, the sole proprietor of Pommery and Greno Ltd of London, and solely responsible for its debts. He was still buoyant; he 'would soon get the old ship on an even keel again.' His employers at Rheims, however, took a different view. They were not prepared to give him any breathing space. And it was at this point that the Guillet brothers stepped in. They were able and willing to settle all the debts without delay, provided they were given the agency. The Polignacs accepted the offer. The London company was obliterated, and André was left without money or employment.

Such is André's account of the affair. Of course there was

more to it than this. By any criterion the way it was done reflects little credit on the proprietors of Pommery; and the conduct of the Guillets is hard to justify. The difficulty in arriving at the truth is accentuated by the fact that, so far as I am aware, nobody else ever put the whole story down on paper; at any rate no record seems to have survived. All that can be done is to piece together such details as can be provided by those who knew the man and know something of the circumstances.

Old associates of André Simon, much as they cherish his memory, are generally agreed that, in matters of finance, he was shrewdly acquisitive and not overburdened with scruple. The view has been expressed that there was much of the French peasant in his make-up. Undoubtedly he made a good thing of the Pommery agency. One old friend of his assures me that at the height of his prosperity he made £1 per case of champagne that he resold, and that he sold 100,000 cases a year. If this is so, it is easy to see that the loss of the agency was a tremendous blow; it is likewise difficult to believe that, even when he had partially settled the losses of 1931, he was left personally destitute.

This helps to explain the part played in André's downfall by the Marquis de Polignac. Melchior had in the past been a good friend to his agent, and he would surely not have behaved with such unfeeling abruptness had he not seen good cause to do so; André was not to blame for the fluctuations of the franc. What return, in fact, had come to Pommery of Rheims from the profit on those 100,000 cases a year sold to British buyers?

It seems certain that André, happy in feathering his own nest, had grown lax in his services to his patrons in Rheims. He was living the Good Life with joyous abandon; but how far did those glorious lunches and dinners, those feasts of pre-phylloxera claret, benefit the firm that employed him to boost its own fortunes? Even when it came to champagne, it was felt that the activities of the London agent did as much to advertise the merits of other brands as he did those of Pommery.

In these circumstances, and with the world slump threatening the economy of France equally with that of Britain, Melchior de Polignac must have felt that loyalty to his old friend was a luxury that his firm could no longer afford. This is not to say that the brutal manner in which the blow was delivered can be condoned.

To André the shock was more moral than material. To be suddenly given the sack after thirty years, in which he had every reason to believe that he enjoyed the complete trust of his patrons, was a humiliation that caused him the deepest distress. What hurt him most of all was that the agents of his fall from grace were friends intimately connected with his own family, one of them the husband of his favourite child, his eldest daughter Jeanne.

How far William, the younger of the two brothers, was responsible for what happened can only be conjectured. But it should be emphasised that Jeanne Rouyer Guillet throughout the sad episode remained completely loyal to her father, as she has been to him and to his memory from that day to this.

As to the financial aspect of the calamity, it was probably not as devastating to André as has sometimes been suggested. He had always lived well, and in recent times quite lavishly. He took the view that, once he had done all that a father could do for the education and well-being of his family, what remained of his income could legitimately be spent on enjoyment and on the Good Life. Nevertheless that income was a large one, and it is hard to believe that, shrewd personal economist that he was, he had not saved enough out of it to face the lean times without despair. It does not appear that his life-style was seriously changed, even temporarily. *Tables of Content* continues to record lavish meals and the best of wines; though from this time on André was more often a guest, less often the host.

At the same time the blow was far from negligible. He was in his mid-fifties, suddenly deprived of employment in the midst of a major national slump, and with no immediate prospect of any amelioration of his financial state. He was, however, buoyant and resilient as ever; he would find something to do, and there were always more books he could write. The goddess Fortuna had always smiled on him before. She was not likely to desert him now.

Nor did she.

Just a month after his dismissal from the Pommery agency, André had an unexpected visitor. A stranger called at Evelyn Mansions, and announced himself as Julian Leacock, a member of a family prominent in the wine trade of Madeira.

The wine of Madeira has, like port, for centuries been particularly associated with the English market. The connection goes back to 1654, when a treaty between the King of Portugal and Oliver Cromwell, then Lord Protector of England, granted special privileges to English merchants who settled in Portugal or Madeira. The principal trade was in red and white wines, but about the middle of the eighteenth century a fortified wine was developed as the characteristic madeira that we know today. There are two main varieties: a dry madeira of a similar type to sherry and a sweet product, often known as Malmsey, which rivals port as a dessert wine. The distinctive quality of madeira is the reputation it enjoys of lasting longer than any other wine, with the possible exception of the very rare Imperial Tokay of Hungary.

The trade flourished and expanded in the eighteenth and nineteenth centuries, and a number of families of English shippers came to eminence as being among the best-known inhabitants of the island. They included the Blandys and the

Leacocks, and it was a scion of the latter house who now called on André.

The proposal that Julian Leacock had to make could hardly have been more attractive. He and his wife were living in London, but had planned to pay a visit to Julian's aged mother in Madeira and at the same time take the opportunity to discuss the shipping business with his brother John, now in charge of the firm. They were due to sail from Southampton in two days' time, but at the last moment one of Julian's sons had been taken ill, and Mrs Leacock decided that she must stay at home and look after him.

Julian was left with two return tickets to Madeira by the Union Castle line. He consulted some friends in the wine trade, and was told that the wine expert André Simon was just now at a loose end and would be the very man to invite to make the trip. The trade in Madeira's wine was in a bad way; demand in England had never been lower. André's advice on how to improve it would be invaluable.

So Julian Leacock went straight to Evelyn Mansions. His suggestion was that André should make use of the second liner ticket, go to Madeira at his expense, and stay for a fortnight as the guest of Mr and Mrs John Leacock, during which time he could study the wine situation on the spot and advise on the future of the trade.

It was a delightful offer, and one after André's own heart; his initial refusal to accept it hardly carries conviction. He could not, he told Leacock, possibly leave his wife in the difficult time they were enduring. But Edith, ebullient as usual, had no such inhibitions. The trip would be the very thing to take her husband's mind off his own troubles, and the complete change would enable him to think over what the future was to hold. He would be a fool not to accept.

André allowed himself to be persuaded. In the New Year he sailed with Julian Leacock to Funchal.

He had caught glimpses of Madeira a number of times

before, but only when his ship put in there on his trips to South Africa. He had never stayed there, and had never paid any particular attention to the wine. Now he made a study of it, and enjoyed himself hugely in the process.

His most memorable experience was that of drinking a madeira that had reached the age of a hundred and forty. Not only was it the oldest wine he had ever tasted, but this particular vintage had an interesting history. The facts of this are related in the little book on madeira that he produced not long after his return home.

The Leacocks were the best of hosts, and they introduced him to all the most important figures in the wine trade. On one of his fleeting visits to Funchal in 1920 he had met the venerable head of the Blandy family, and now he was invited to dinner by Blandy's widow. The meal was a splendid one, and André ventured to tell his hostess how wonderful was the madeira they were drinking, and how grateful he was to her.

'Of course', was her reply, 'I am giving you the best I have, but it is not the best there is in the island. Uncle Michael has the best there is: he does not drink it, he does not give it away, and he will not sell it.' She added that the possessor of the great wine was about to celebrate his ninety-third birthday.

'Uncle Michael' was Dr Michael Grabham, 'the grand old man of Madeira'. André met him a few days later through the good offices of Sir Stephen Gaselee, the classical scholar and librarian of the House of Lords, who was an old friend and a fellow member of the Saintsbury Club. Gaselee spent a holiday every year in Madeira, and when André told him about the 1792 wine, of which rather strangely he did not know, he arranged for the two to meet at lunch. André was enchanted with the old man, a hale and hearty nonagenarian, and that the attraction was mutual was shown by the fact that Grabham invited both him and Gaselee to his birthday celebration; and there he opened for them a bottle of his illustrious madeira.

André tells its story, as related by Dr Grabham:

'This wine,' the old Doctor told me, 'was made in 1792, a very good year indeed, and, by the way, the year when my father was born. When, in 1815, Napoleon I called at Madeira, on his way farther south, to St Helena, this 1792 wine was picked out as likely to become very fine, with age, and it was bought for the fallen Emperor, to help him forget the duress of exile. But, as you know, they found out that he suffered from some gastric trouble – some said that it was cancer of the stomach – and they would not let him drink this wine. As a matter of fact, the Emperor died in 1820, and this 1792 was hardly ready by then. The curious thing about it was that nobody had paid for the wine. That is to say, the English Consul at Funchal, a Mr Veitch, had paid the merchant who had put the wine on board His Britannic Majesty's ship, in 1815, but he, Veitch, had never been able to get the money refunded. So he did the next best thing. He claimed the pipe of 1792 as his own, and he got it back in Madeira, in 1822, when he sold it to Charles Blandy. His son, John Blandy, bottled the wine in 1840, and that happens to be the year when I was born. I married his daughter; that is how the wine came to me, and why I can give it to you to-day.'

André describes the 1792 madeira as 'perfect as regards colour, bouquet and flavour, but even more remarkable, if possible, on account of its pedigree'.

It was not quite the end of the story. When Gaselee was returning to London that year, Dr Grabham, no doubt reflecting that at his time of life there was no point in keeping the wine, presented him with what was believed to be his last case. André was able to enjoy the venerable wine again in Gaselee's company.

With regard to the more serious objectives of the trip,

André earned his passage and the hospitality he enjoyed by studying all aspects of Madeira's wine production. Madeira was going through a bad patch. In earlier days the wine had enjoyed large sales in Britain, largely through the personal influence of George IV, who as Prince Regent spread its popularity as his favourite tipple. Later in the nineteenth century it became even more popular in America, and it was there that the biggest trade was done up to the time of the First World War. But then came prohibition, and the market closed; a good fortified wine was not the stuff of which profitable bootleg liquor was made. The market did not revive when the prohibition madness ended.

Meanwhile sales had fallen off badly in Britain. The problem now was how to restore its popularity there. Madeira is a small island, with no great vineyards such as abound in the wine districts of France and other European countries. Most of the Madeira shippers now had other interests which took precedence of the dwindling wine trade; none of them individually could afford a publicity campaign to boost its sales abroad.

In these circumstances André advised the shippers to put their heads, their wine and their money together and embark on a united effort. The Blandys, the Leacocks and the rest were in unanimous agreement, and were only too pleased to entrust the campaign to André Simon.

So it came about that, when he returned to London, and was met by Edith, André was able to tell her that he was the chairman of the Madeira Wine Association, which had been formed to bring madeira back into fashion. He had a job once more.

André was the first to admit that the campaign achieved no great success. He personally did what he could, enlisting the help of his friends in the wine trade. He proclaimed the virtues of the wine, and persuaded some of the leading hotels and restaurants to put the madeiras he provided on their wine lists. But, as he recorded, 'there they remained; there was practically no demand, nor any funds for a publicity campaign.' The time was not ripe. There was 'deep depression in the wine trade, when there were over two million unemployed on the dole, and when noble lords and not so noble bookmakers drank beer instead of champagne at the Embassy Club.'

André got more satisfaction from his literary labours. *Tables of Content* came out in the same year, 1933, but a more profitable venture was Constable's Wine Library.

Once again the idea came from Michael Sadleir, who proposed the publication of a series of short and inexpensive books on various wines; each was to run to some 30,000 words, and to cater not for the wine trade but for the members of the public who liked their wine and wanted to learn about it. André was invited to edit the series and to choose authors for the various books.

He promptly accepted, and with his usual alacrity had the first volume ready before the end of 1933. It was on madeira, the wine fresh in his mind; but André wrote only half of it. He found 15,000 words enough to comprise all he had to say about madeira. The rest was supplied by Elizabeth Craig, who wrote on the use of the wine in cooking and in sauces. The title of the little book was *Madeira: Wine, Cakes and Sauce*.

André wrote two more books in the series, on champagne and on port, these being by himself alone. Both were out before the end of the following year. The other authors he selected were Warner Allen for sherry, Maurice Healy for the wines of Bordeaux, Stephen Gwynn for burgundy, Hugh Rudd for hock and moselle, and Elizabeth Craig for wine in the kitchen.

All the books were published in 1933 or 1934, and sales were brisk. The most successful was Healy's.

In the meantime the Madeira Wine Association had folded up. It never made its mark, and after nine months its sponsors in the island decided that the experiment was not worth the money expended.

For the second time André had lost a job. This time it did not worry him. He had found a new interest – one that was to take up almost the whole of his attention for the remainder of his working life.

The Wine and Food Society evolved from a confluence of André's dearest interests. It enabled him to continue to enjoy the best of food and wine, and at the same time to proclaim and spread his gospel of gastronomy. But the whole conception arose from his predilection for journalism and his dedication to the printed word.

Germinating in his mind for some time had been the idea of starting a wine magazine in which he could put forward his own views. He knew well from experience how quickly books on wine, dealing as they had to do with successive vintages, became out of date. A periodical providing continuous discussion of events and situations as they occurred was the solution that commended itself to him. Now, when he had no very serious work to occupy his time, it seemed that the opportunity had come. The chief obstacle, of course, was lack of adequate capital; but André was not one to be put off by so paltry a consideration.

He decided to consult one of his acquaintances in the world of journalism, and the pundit he chose was J. L. Garvin, the pontifical editor of the *Observer*. He arranged to visit Garvin at his house at Beaconsfield, and over lunch the two discussed the prospects. Garvin was not sanguine on the possibility of a magazine devoted to wine; it would not attract a sufficient readership. Others had given similar advice, but Garvin had a further suggestion. Why should not André form some sort of 'eat and drink society' on the lines of the

First Edition Club, the members of which would finance with their subscriptions the publication of a magazine which would then be distributed free to them, as was the *Book Collector's Quarterly* to the club named?

The First Edition Club still existed, though its grandiose days were over; it functioned from an office in Little Russell Street, and its guiding light was still A. J. A. Symons. Garvin's advice sent André hot-foot to Symons with the suggestion of collaboration, and his young friend welcomed the project with the optimism and enthusiasm with which he was wont to greet any new and enterprising idea. His immediate reaction is described in *By Request*:

> 'Eat' was the spark that fired A.J.'s inflammable imagination. 'Food,' he called out triumphantly, 'food is news. With two million unemployed existing on the dole; with restrictions, frustration and difficulties all round, food is first-class news. We'll tell people how to make the most of what little food they can afford to buy. We'll show them how to do it. We'll open a restaurant for our members, a luncheon and dinner club, with the finest food at the lowest prices. We'll have a thousand members within a year and ten thousand in two or three years. And we'll give them a magazine, a monthly bulletin with the right recipes for everything in season month by month.'

A.J., as André had good reason to know, was apt to let his enthusiasm run away with him; but André was enthusiastic too, and the younger man's ideas appealed to him. From the first the two men were in accord, and a partnership was soon in the making. Events were to show that, in this case at least, Symons's dreams were capable of fulfilment. The restaurant idea was soon dropped, and the production of a monthly magazine was judged too ambitious. But the rest of A.J.'s estimate of future prospects was not too far wide of the mark.

Finance was certainly a problem, and Symons himself insisted that it would be impossible to launch the magazine before the society had at least five hundred paying members. Both prospective partners, however, were optimistic. A.J. was confident of finding wealthy backers among his influential acquaintances. André was less sanguine, but he too had the good will of important friends in the wine trade.

The name of the new organisation was a matter of argument. Various suggestions were made, culminating in A.J.'s proposal that it should be called the Food and Wine Society. Here André was adamant. In a gastronomic alliance wine was the senior partner; in the perfect meal food provided the frame within which great wine could shine. The new body must give undisputed precedence to wine. Symons eventually allowed himself to be persuaded.

Other points of contention were ironed out, and on 20 October 1933 the Wine and Food Society came into existence. An agreement was drawn up, according to which André Simon was declared the first president of the society and A. J. A. Symons the first secretary. It was a straightforward private agreement between the two men, and any profits that arose were to be divided equally between them. A.J. was to deal with the routine business and correspondence, and to provide the premises and staff; both were the same as those of the First Edition Club. André's part was to arrange all the society's luncheons, dinners and tastings, while he was also to be solely responsible for editing the society's magazine when it should be found possible to publish it.

The founding partners were perfectly confident that they could run the society without any outside assistance. After a little discussion, however, it was decided that there would be no harm in recruiting a body of influential connoisseurs of wine and food whose names, with one or two titles thrown in, would look well on the society's stationery when the new association was launched. So an 'advisory council' was formed, subject to the private agreement between the founders that the advice of the advisory council should never be asked. Professor Henry Armstrong and the Dowager Lady Swaythling, both enthusiastic gastronomes and old friends of André, were the first two members of the council. They were followed by Maurice Healy and Sir Francis Colchester-Wemyss; others were H. Warner Allen, Marcel Boulestin, Elizabeth Craig, Ambrose Heath, J. C. Squire, G. B. Stern, Lord Moynihan and Vyvyan Holland, the brilliant son of Oscar Wilde. André would have liked to add the names of those two old stalwarts Ian Campbell and Francis Berry; but neither was willing to serve. They felt that it would be unwise to include names so closely associated with the wine trade.

Social functions, the prime *raison d'être* of the Wine and Food Society, were from the first known simply as 'meetings'; the first such meeting was held at the Café Royal on 14 November 1933. It took the form of an Alsatian luncheon; René Dopff, of Colmar and Riquewihr, anxious to develop the market for his firm's wines, offered André a selection of the best of them. Members of the newly-born society were thus able to enjoy a five-course lunch with a 1929 Riesling, a Gewürztraminer of the same year and a 1928 Grande Réserve Traminer – all at a cost of 10s. 6d. a head, service included. André was in the chair, and 212 members and guests attended. It was a splendid start for the Society.

The Alsatian lunch was followed a month later by a tasting, in the Society's Little Russell Street office, of the wines of Madeira, provided of course by the Madeira Wine Association, then still in existence. For the large sum of half a crown each, members sampled what André later described as 'a great many different wines, some very cheap for Sauce Madère, some good enough and reasonable in price, others from fine to great in both quality and cost, and finally a few quite priceless wines of the late eighteenth century, not for sale'. Quantity for tasting was unlimited.

In January 1934 came the first full dinner of the Society, when 384 members and friends sat down to a 'Savoyard' meal at the Savoy. The cost was a guinea a head, and the finest of the region's dishes were served with wines from the Rhône. The Dowager Lady Swaythling presided, and in proposing the toast of the Society she revealed that membership had risen to 494 and that people were joining from all ranks of life and from all professions. The Society's aim was, as she put it, not only to indulge in wining and dining but to improve the standard of cooking throughout the country so that it could compare favourably with that to be found abroad.

The Wine and Food Society was in fact going from strength to strength. The venture had been timed to perfection. Everywhere there was weariness with the austerity induced by the sterling crisis. A society devoted to the civilised pleasures of the table caught the popular mood. At the same time the success achieved so early took the founding partners by surprise. It was what they had hoped for but had hardly expected.

In the spring of 1934 came the first issue of the promised magazine, *Wine and Food*, André's brain-child of which he had dreamed so fervently. Announced as 'a gastronomical quarterly', it was produced in an elegantly dignified format, priced at 2s. 6d. The moving hand throughout was André's. He of course wrote the editorial, recounting the history of the formation of the Wine and Food Society; but he also contributed an article on the 1933 vintage in France, Germany and Portugal, and described the first five meetings of the Society (two more had by now been held). Other contributors were A. J. A. Symons, G. B. Stern, Henry Armstrong and Ernest Oldmeadow.

Before the end of the year, membership of the Society had passed the thousand-mark. In the summer the second number of *Wine and Food* duly appeared; Horace Annesley Vachell, Stephen Gaselee and Marcel Boulestin were now contributors. In an enthusiastic editorial André alluded to the rapid increase in membership and enlarged on prospects for the future:

> 'What is going to happen if we continue to grow?' is a question that is beginning to be asked; 'And where shall we accommodate our increasing numbers? Will not the demonstration dinners and lunches suffer if they become too large?'
>
> There is no need for concern. Our Meetings will not be allowed to become unwieldy. Future functions will, when necessary, be duplicated; Members will be given a choice of dates, on any of which they will be able to sample the fare provided and bring guests. The maximum number permitted at each Meeting will probably vary between one hundred and three hundred according to the circumstances and the place chosen.

It was an ambitious programme, particularly when it is remembered that lunches and dinners were not the only functions of the Society. Tours of continental wine districts were arranged at vintage time; tastings and lectures on gastronomic subjects were planned, and it was decided to hold an annual conference at which practical gastronomy would take at least as prominent a place as the spoken word. The conferences were to be in October, to mark successive anniversaries of the formation of the Society, and each year in a different county for the purpose of spreading the gospel of gastronomy throughout the country. André was on the crest of the wave, and had no fears for the future of the venture that was first and foremost his.

The first annual conference, which opened at Brighton on

20 October 1934, the actual anniversary, was a memorable occasion, embodying as it did by far the most ambitious 'meeting' yet attempted. Brighton's municipal authorities put at the disposal of the Society no less a building than the Royal Pavilion, sacred to the memory of George IV and the Regency, and there André and his followers planned to hold a Regency banquet that should do full justice to the 'First Gentleman of Europe', who had been the leading *bon vivant* of his day. In preparation for the great event the autumn issue of *Wine and Food* took the form of a special number devoted to the subject of Carême, the nineteenth century's pre-eminent chef, whose patrons in addition to the Prince Regent had included Napoleon Bonaparte and the Czar Alexander I of Russia; the centenary of his death had occurred in the year of the Society's inauguration. It was an imposing number. André was naturally to the fore, providing a learned biographical article on Carême, while Duff Cooper, making his début as a contributor to *Wine and Food*, wrote on the great chef's association with Talleyrand.

The meeting itself was on a tremendous scale; Julian Symons, in his biography of his brother, describes it as 'the most sumptuous and elaborate banquet held in Brighton for more than a hundred years'. It was modelled with great care on dishes actually served by Carême to the Regent, and consisted of forty-two courses, with sixteen specially chosen wines and liqueurs, provided in two 'services' in the manner of the early nineteenth century. Some of the dishes, writes Julian Symons, 'like the boar's head and the two models in iced sugar of *"Le Temple de l'Amour"* and *"Le Frégate 'La Gourmande'"*, were designed for admiration rather than consumption; but although one person present denied indignantly that the meal had been "the banquet of a glutton or a wine-bibber", being merely "the dinner of people who took trouble to ensure that everything was artistically right", another was astonished by a thin young man on his left who sampled two of the four kinds of soup, all the six *hors d'oeuvres*, both sorts of fish, the veal and the chicken among the four entrées, and even the neglected boar's head, in the first service alone.'

Clearly it was no mean repast. 'Two hundred people, who had paid two guineas each, sat down to eat in the vast E-shaped Chinese dining room, lighted by thousands of tallow candles in eighty great candelabra.' Before the dinner, after Symons had given a happy report of the first year of the Society, members visited the Pavilion's kitchens and saw the dishes they were to taste being prepared on the great revolving spits before a huge fire which had not been lit for half a century. The meal itself took two hours and a half to serve, and afterwards, in the majestic music room, there was a concert of chamber music by Arne, Boyce, Handel and Vivaldi.

The Pavilion banquet constituted the eleventh meeting of the Society. When, in the winter number, *Wine and Food* got around to reporting the event, it solemnly recorded that 'the lateness of the hour made it necessary for a number of the diners to forgo the final pleasure of the concert'. It was the general view that the lateness of the hour was not the only factor hampering musical appreciation.

The whole affair did just what André hoped it would; it put the Wine and Food Society on the map. The lavishness of the entertainment provided, coupled with the splendid setting and its historical significance, caught the public imagination, and many who would not otherwise have heard of the Society pricked up their ears and took an interest. Gastronomical revolution was on the way, and its undisputed leader was André Louis Simon.

Little more than a year after the one major setback of his career, he was back at work with his future clear before him. And the work on which he had embarked was of a nature completely after his own heart, more congenial to him than the mere selling of champagne had ever been.

It was to remain the central interest of his life for the next thirty years and more.

–8–

Wine and Food

FROM 1933 onwards, until the yet far distant date when he would finally feel that the time had come for him to say goodbye to London, the story of André Simon's life is inseparable from that of the Wine and Food Society. He had found a goal which embodied his deepest interests and his dearest aims, and he pursued that goal with single-minded enthusiasm, an enthusiasm none the less ardent for the marks it bore of a courtly manner and unhurried gait that were the unfailing guise of his bearing towards the world.

The six years before civilisation once again burst into flame were for him placid years. His private life was happy. He was no longer worried about the future. He had a secure occupation, and it was one that enabled him to devote himself with untroubled devotion to his self-imposed mission of furthering the revolution in the development of good living which was now under way and of which he was the accepted leader.

It was never his idea that the Wine and Food Society should remain static in the rôle it had assumed at the start. He meant it to expand not only throughout the length and breadth of the British Isles, but into other lands as well. And the English-speaking regions were the first objective. André had never visited the United States. That country was certainly, as he wrote in *In the Twilight*, no place for him during the era of the lunacy of Prohibition. But now the Volstead Act had been repealed, and 'a ray of real sunshine came across the Atlantic'. From now on America began to play an important part in his thinking. It seemed to him that in that great territory there was a public of almost unlimited dimensions to provide virgin soil for the development of the doctrine of the Good Life on a scale so far hardly thought of. America was a land of sun, a land which was already making its own wines – wines that needed only expert handling to enable them to take their place beside the more venerable vintages of Europe. But beyond that the citizens of the United States had plenty to discover about the wines, and the food too, that had grown with the centuries in the maturer regions of the Old World. And Americans, as everybody knew, were always eager to learn, always receptive to unfamiliar ideas. André resolved to cross the Atlantic at the earliest opportunity.

That opportunity was not long in coming. But before it came, before even the great day of the Regency Banquet, an event took place at home in the history of the Wine and Food Society which should not be passed over in silence. This was the visit of the Society to the home of its president, an outdoor luncheon in the lovely garden that André had created in Sussex.

Some two hundred members of the Society assembled at Little Hedgecourt on 7 July 1934. The fortune that so seldom deserted André Simon was much in evidence; it was a blazing summer day, and the garden was at its best. 'An English Day' was the theme of the event. The fare, as listed subsequently in *Wine and Food*, was:

Lobster Salad

Roast Surrey Fowl

York Ham

Glazed Ox Tongue

Pigeon Pie
Veal and Ham Pie

Roast Fore-Rib of Beef

Potato Salad   Green Salad

Raspberries and Cream
Meringues

Charlotte Russe

The English theme extended to the drinks. This was perhaps the only meal ever organised by the Wine and Food Society at which no wine was served. Instead there were Whitbread's India Pale Ale, Watney's Export India Pale Ale and Barclay's London Lager. And those attending were given a leaflet of notes on the best ways of drinking beer.

It was a happy day, and one that lingered long in the memories of all who were there; particularly in those of André and Edith and their family.

It was enough, perhaps, to anchor him to England. But America still loomed, and before that came France. For the next month André spent with one of his dearest friends. 'Alice Delysia', we read in *By Request*, 'had a heart of gold; she also had a delightful villa at Bidart, near Biarritz, called La Malika, and it was at La Malika that my wife and I, Jeanne and Emile, our eldest daughter and grandson, spent the month of August, 1934.' And it was at La Malika that André received just the visit he needed to encourage him to go ahead with his plans.

Jean Couprie, secretary-general of the Commission d'Exportation des Vins de France, had come from Paris specially to see him. At Bordeaux he was joined by Roger Descas, president of the Bordeaux Shippers' Association, and together the two of them bearded André Simon at La Malika. Couprie explained their mission. The repeal of the Volstead Act had raised the hopes of the French wine trade. 'A great many wine-merchants and officials had rushed across the

Atlantic, the first at their own expense and the others at the expense of various Government Departments or trade organisations. But it appeared that all of them had been greatly disappointed: they had found it extremely easy to spend a lot of money but also extremely difficult, not to say impossible, to get orders or even to get Americans interested in the wines of France.' In these circumstances Couprie and his colleagues, like others before them, had recourse to André Simon, whose presence in France seemed providential. Couprie, in fact, had been commissioned by the Comité de Propagande to find out if André would be prepared to go to America on 'what might be called a lectures-cum-banquets tour' that would make Americans realise how fortunate they were to have once again the chance of drinking French wines, the finest the world had to offer.

André's first answer, as it had been in the project of the Madeira trip, was an emphatic 'No'. He pointed out that Couprie was asking him to do what, as he had himself explained, a number of others had tried to do and failed. What chance was there that he could do better? Moreover he was fully occupied with the Wine and Food Society and with *Wine and Food*, both of which he was working hard to make a lasting success.

Once again the initial refusal needs explanation. André had already decided that he wanted to visit the United States, and here was a splendid opportunity. As for the Wine and Food Society, A. J. A. Symons was eminently capable of carrying on its affairs single-handed, and with his energy and enthusiasm would obviously be glad to do so.

The real reason, however, why André was not eager to accept the offer was that the mission was too limited in its objective. He had his own vision of what he wanted to do; it was to spread the gospel of gastronomy among the cultured public of the New World. To make the trip as a representative of a group of French wine-merchants would be to hamper him in his wider aim.

This is borne out by the sequel, as told in André's own words:

Of course, Couprie and Descas had not come all the way to Bidart to take the first no as a final answer and they pressed me to think it over. 'Well,' I said to them, 'I will go, if you are so keen that I should, but I will go on my own terms, and that is: if it is agreed that I will not boost French wines, but do my best to pass on to a few of the more cultured and influential American citizens in each of the great cities my own faith in *Wine*, not French wines, mark you, but *Wine* as the fairway of a truly civilized mode of living, far more wholesome than iced water and infinitely safer than ardent spirits. If I can convince them that *Wine* is the best partner of food and that there is no really gracious way of living without the right wine served with the right food, I will beg of them to spread the good news around them, to form local Wine and Food Societies for the education of the taste of their fellow-citizens.'

Not long after, I was asked to attend a full meeting of the Comité in Paris, and I was told that they all agreed that I should go as soon as ever I could arrange it, with my wife, and do my best in my own way.

As usual, André had got his own way; he had been invited to make the trip on his own terms, a trip that promised to be a delightful holiday for himself and Edith.

They booked their passage by the French liner *Paris*, due to sail from Le Havre for New York on 15 November, and in the meantime André got in touch with such influential figures in American wine circles as he could trace. One of these was Frank Schoonmaker who with Tom Marvel of the *New York Herald* in Paris had just written 'an excellent book on wines', and an illuminating correspondence ensued. A letter written by Marvel on 10 October shows how far his views accorded with André's own:

My dear Mr Simon:

You will receive, as soon as it comes from the press, next month, a copy of 'The Complete Wine Book', by Mr Frank Schoonmaker and myself, with our compliments. It should be of especial interest to you in view of your coming campaign for wine in America.

My friend, M. Leon Douarche, of the Office International du Vin, says you are leaving for the United States very soon. I think you will be interested in getting in touch with my colleague, Mr Schoonmaker, and I am sure he will enjoy meeting you.

We are both very much interested in making wine popular in our country. I have even started on plans for launching a consumers' wine group there, a draft prospectus of which I enclose.

You will see from my outline that we are emphasizing first, our native wines. Our country is not only a potentially large wine consumer; it is also a wine growing region of great possibilities. And it is my experience that a wine drinking country is also, and invariably, a wine growing country – in other words, the countries that drink the most wine drink mostly their home product. All of which is quite natural.

And this is quite in line with your own interests, however much to the contrary it may appear. For we must get Americans used to drinking, not the wines of this place or that, but simply Wine – any wine. And the easiest, the most logical place to start is right at home.

There is no question of native wines competing with foreign vintages. We insist that they are different – in a class by themselves – and to that end we shall fight, as we have fought in our own book, against the use of European names for American wines. We shall continue the fight until we have won – not through legislation but through education of the consumer – honest American names for honest American wines. Here again, we are helping the importer.

I shall be in New York in December, at which time I hope to have the pleasure of meeting you and of aiding you in every way at my disposal.

With best wishes, I am,
Yours very truly,
Tom Marvel

The New York Herald
Paris

The draft prospectus for a proposed Wine Society which Marvel enclosed with his letter dealt first and foremost with the question of the labelling of native wines. 'American wines', it opened, 'suffer from the world's worst inferiority complex. Growers and distributors of American wines refuse to allow their product to go before the Consumer under honest, American names. They have given us, since Repeal, nothing but third-rate, standardised wines, at ridiculously high prices, under labels that bear false European designations, such as "Chablis", "Sherry", 'Burgundy", etc, that tell us, in most cases, nothing of the year of vintage, of the grapes from which they are made, or of the vineyard region they come from.'

The proposed society was announced as aiming at a programme of six main points:

1. To encourage the proper use and enjoyment of all wines, foreign and domestic, that were honestly labelled, honestly produced and honestly priced.
2. To awaken among Americans an appreciation of

their own wines as distinctive regional productions: not imitations of European wines.

3. To encourage the development of vineyards in the United States, private and commercial, along regional lines.

4. To provide a source of expert and unbiased advice and information on all questions concerning wine.

5. To work for legislation recognising natural wine as a food, the free and normal use of which was conducive to temperance.

6. To raise the standard of cooking by encouraging hotels and restaurants which served meals cooked with wine and with which sound and honest wines at moderate prices were served.

This was a programme after André's heart, and he looked forward more than ever to his transatlantic tour. Marvel and Schoonmaker, he saw, would be the most valuable of allies.

Preparations went forward smoothly. Two days before André and Edith sailed they were entertained by the Wine and Food Society to a farewell banquet at the Savoy. It was a memorable occasion, graced by representatives of all the wine-producing countries of Europe; the ambassadors of Spain and Portugal attended in person; the others were represented by senior delegates from the various embassies. There were 495 members and guests present, and Colonel Ian Campbell presided. Dishes were planned to give examples of cooking from a wide variety of nations, and seven different brands of champagne were served. It was a send-off worthy of the guest of honour.

André and Edith duly embarked at Plymouth in the *Paris* on 15 November 1934, 'on a cold and boisterous November night'. But a few days later they were sailing happily up the

Hudson River 'on a crisp, clear, sunny November afternoon'.

Like many another traveller, André was thrilled by his first sight of the New York skyline. The houses, he was to write later, 'are simply wonderful. That is, from outside. New York's skyline as you come up the Hudson upon a sunny winter's afternoon is extraordinarily fascinating. The City seems to be sitting up, or rather standing up on tip-toe, awaiting you.' The skyscrapers 'are huge, but they are beautiful and perfectly in their place. That is probably the secret of their looking so handsome; they are in the right place, they fit in with the whole layout of New York, its compactness, its individuality and its symmetry.' On their arrival in the city he and Edith were warmly welcomed by his admirers, and when they settled down on the thirty-fourth floor of the Hotel Pierre everything pointed to a successful trip.

Nevertheless this first visit to New York was a disappointment. In spite of the good offices of Frank Schoonmaker, André sought in vain the type of wine-lover he was looking for, 'the people who could and would have made a success of a New York Wine and Food Society on the lines which I had in mind'.

America's greatest city was in fact not yet ready for the gastronomic revolution. Only just emerging from the blight of Prohibition, it was immersed in a flood of spirits and cocktails; the doctrine of good wine with meals had no message for it. People who venerated the good things of life in the world of André Simon were few and without influence.

Food was as little appreciated as wine. In an article entitled 'First American Impressions', published later in *Wine and Food*, André summed up his conclusions:

. . . Now we are coming to the greatest tragedy of all, the tragedy of missed opportunities and wrecked chances . . .

The tragedy is that in a country where there is more cattle, grain and vegetables than in any other, as well as an enormous variety of fish, even if only very little game, the standard of feeding should be so low, or it would be more exact to say so utterly wrong. The tragedy is that in a country where more money is spent than in any other in the world on research, education and the application of scientific discoveries to everyday necessities, people should feed so unscientifically, so stupidly – there is really, to my mind, no nearer word to the truth than stupidly – as the average American feeds or is fed. He or she does not trouble to think about the value, taste, preparation and effects of food any more than children do in the nursery. Rather less. Children know what they like. Most grown-ups do not even know that much . . .

The average American probably spends more than the average citizen of any other country in the world upon food and drink, but he certainly is less well nourished than the ordinary peasant class in any part of Europe. To say nothing of the little French bourgeois whose income is half that of a New York elevator boy, and yet feeds far better than a Chicago packing millionaire.

It was a devastating indictment. But André saw hope for the future:

Of course, a great deal of the blame for the deplorable conditions at present so general in America can surely be traced to the blight of Prohibition. The men and women in their early thirties to-day have grown up in the foul air of deceit, gangsters and bath-tub gin. The hip-flask was the god of their youth. How can they be expected to turn to the shrine where Bacchus holds his court? They like hard liquor better. They preface what is to be dinner with a few 'old-fashioned' cocktails and come to table in a semi-dazed condition, not wanting any food, but craving for cigarettes, which poison the air for their fellow-guests and burn holes in the hostess's best table-cloth. Wine to them, in their state, is nauseating; they want a high-ball or something with a kick in it. They are beyond reform as beyond civilization altogether, however smart may be the cut of their coat or their own value of themselves. Happily, there are others. There are many who are afraid of hard liquor, as well they may be if they have eyes to see what hard liquor has done for so many of their friends. They will be, probably, the majority of the new converts to the cause of wine, and with a growing appreciation of wine will come a greater appreciation of better food, food prepared with greater care, served with more intelligence and enjoyed at greater leisure. It is with them and their friends, the friends whom they will convince of the importance of eating and drinking sensibly, that rests the hope of the revolution that is so badly needed in the United States, needed so that the many millions of unfortunate people who at present live on their nerves and pills, can take due advantage of the admirable supplies of foodstuffs and wines which they have ignored or so badly used in the past.

Happily New York is not the whole of the United States, and in other centres it was a different story. André and Edith left early in December for Boston, and there, where they were the guests of a noted wine-lover, Sohier Welch, and his wife, they found an enthusiasm for the Good Life which had been so conspicuously lacking in the bigger city. 'Much to our surprise and delight', wrote André in *In the Twilight*, 'we found that our Boston friends had more to teach us than we could teach them. Sohier Welch, Gus Loring, Charlie Codman and a few more had already started a dining club which they called Le Club des Arts Gastronomiques. All were true wine lovers, and although Charlie Codman was in charge of the wine department of Boston's finest department store, it only meant that he knew more about wine than his friends; he was as unprejudiced as any of them.'

The moving spirit of the group was a lady, Theodora Codman. 'She was the dynamic and highly intelligent wife of Charlie Codman, and she realized at once that a Boston Wine and Food Society would do far more for the recognition and appreciation of wine than the dinners of the Club des Arts Gastronomiques for a few men only.' And it was through her efforts that the first American chapter of the Wine and Food Society was formed. 'Gus Loring was the President, benevolent, amiable, Pickwickian somewhat and lovable, but Theodora was the Hon. Secretary, quick, efficient, the "no nonsense" type of woman who gets things done, and well done, but does not expect and rarely gets a thank you.'

So it was that it was at Boston that the Wine and Food Society secured its first real footing in the United States; and the Boston chapter has remained a bulwark of the Society from that day to this.

The next port of call was Chicago, where the travellers were met by Arnold Shircliffe, 'a chef by profession, a book-lover by disposition, and brimming over with the love of and faith in his art'. The Chicago visit, however, was not the success that the Boston one had been. André had had high hopes of meeting another Theodora Codman in Suzette Dewey, who had written a book on wine and who with her husband Peter paid an annual visit to France; they had a house in Normandy.

. . . A Chicago Chapter of the Society with Suzette Dewey as Hon. Secretary would have brought together many if not most of the much travelled and highly cultured men and women of Illinois around Chicago. But it was not to be. They entertained us generously on our arrival but told us that they were leaving Chicago very shortly for

Washington as Mr Dewey was now a senator. With greater haste than sense, I asked Arnold Shircliffe to take charge of a Chicago Chapter of the Society. He was a Birmingham-born American citizen with a rather important job in the catering trade. As a subscriber to one or other of the Wine Trade journals published in London, he had read about the Wine and Food Society and had sent his three dollars to become a member; he was the first member the Society had in the United States, and he had written to me, when we were in New York, asking me to let him know when I would be in Chicago; which, naturally, I did. He could not have been kinder to us nor worked harder for the Society, but he was not really the right type for the job . . .

In what ways Shircliffe fell short of what was required we are not told; but clearly André did not regard the formation of the Chicago chapter as one of the Society's brightest hopes.

The stay in Chicago was short. André and Edith wanted to get to the sunshine of California, and a week before Christmas they arrived at San Francisco. There they were met by Ernest Guy, who before the war had been Melchior de Polignac's private secretary and was now Commercial Counsellor in California. Guy, who was married to a cousin of André's, introduced them to members of the Cercle Français and to local wine enthusiasts such as Harold Price and Bertram Alanson, and soon there was a flourishing San Francisco chapter of the Wine and Food Society in being with Harold Price as its keen honorary secretary, a chapter destined to grow in importance and prosperity with the years. The visitors toured Georges de Latour's vineyards and winery at Beaulieu, which Latour and his wife 'had managed somehow to carry on during the Prohibition years'. On 9 January 1935, the night before they left San Francisco for Los Angeles, they gave a farewell dinner at the St Francis Hotel: 'Champagne and hors d'oeuvres in an ante-room,

then a Bisque de Homard and a 1929 Riquewihr Traminer; a
fine fowl *à l'ivoire*, with a 1923 Clos de Larnage from the
Rhône; a saddle of lamb Jardinière, with a 1926 Château
Lagrange (St Julien) shipped by Calvet; a Foie Gras de
Strasbourg, with a 1926 Clos de Bèze; and last, l'Ananas
glacé voilé à l'Orientale, with a 1917 Château Rayne-
Vigneau.'

At Los Angeles, however, there was a setback. Edith had
caught a chill in San Francisco, and in the excitement of the
tour had not taken enough care of herself. Arrived at their
Los Angeles hotel, she developed pneumonia, and for a time
was seriously ill. She stayed in the hotel, but had to have
attention from day and night nurses. According to André she
would have died of double pneumonia had it not been for the
skill and devotion of Dr Pepper, the hotel doctor.

In spite of his wife's illness, and the worry it entailed,
André was not inactive. Once again he was introduced to
some influential wine-lovers, and he found time to set the ball
rolling for the foundation of a Southern California chapter of
the Society. Then they moved to Palm Springs, where Edith
was able to enjoy a short period of rest and convalescence.

Soon she was on her feet again, and could move with her
husband to New Orleans, where, writes André, 'the tradition
of gastronomy and *la joie de vivre* is probably older than
anywhere else in the United States'. A New Orleans branch
of the Wine and Food Society was immediately started, and
on 11 February André and Edith were present at the first
'meeting', held *Chez Antoine*.

So back to New York, where the travellers spent their final
week before returning to England. Here too the position was
transformed. André's enthusiasm had borne fruit. In the
short period that had elapsed a New York chapter had been
formed, and its president was Henry W. Taft, brother of the
former President of the United States. Neither he nor his
associates, says André, knew anything about wine, 'but they

could trust implicitly the counsels and guidance of Freddie Wildman, a really knowledgeable wine lover and wine-merchant'.

And so this first American tour, in spite of misgivings initially felt, ended as a triumphant success. The Wine and Food Society was well and truly launched in America; chapters were in being in most of the most important cities; in New York, Boston, Chicago, San Francisco, Los Angeles and New Orleans. The doctrine of the Good Life was being preached throughout the country; the revolution was under way.

It was the first of many such visits. Later in 1935, André went again to the United States, this time travelling alone and by air. The tour was more extensive but less thorough than the first; he 'visited a dozen or more cities, gave dinners and talks, had many promises'. New chapters of the Society were formed in Kansas City and Baltimore.

There were four more visits during the remaining years of peace. The last was in May 1939, when André sailed in the *Normandie*, 'the finest passenger ship ever built since Noah's Ark'. He was immensely impressed with the food served in the great liner, which compared favourably with anything he enjoyed on land.

During these last years of peace, in the intervals between the visits to America, André's time was mainly taken up with the Wine and Food Society. He was, however, feeling the pinch financially, and to supplement his income took on, in 1936, an engagement with a firm of advertising practitioners, Mather and Crowther. He was employed mainly in an advis-ory capacity, to draft or amend advertisements. The engage-ment lasted two years, but it would not appear that André gave very valuable service. 'I am afraid', he confessed him-self, 'that Mather and Crowther gave me far more than I was able to give them.' What they gave him, apart from a salary to augment his income from the Wine and Food Society, was the use of an office to himself at their premises overlooking the Savoy Chapel garden. This at least was valuable to him. The offices in Little Russell Street, where A. J. A. Symons conducted the affairs of the First Edition Club as well as those of the Wine and Food Society, were too cramped for him to work out his plans in detail and design his literary activities.

He gave his full attention to the management of the Society. After the first flush of its success in the early years there was something of a slump; 'the number of members who defaulted or resigned was greater than the number of new members'. But there was no real decline. Up to the outbreak of war the Society continued to be a highly popular institution, which had plainly come to stay.

The editorship of *Wine and Food* was taken with intense seriousness. The journal was André's own creation, and he worked with all his energy to make it worthy of his ideals. He induced some of the best-known authors of the day to write for it. The names of Hilaire Belloc, Vyvyan Holland, Alec Waugh, Louis Golding, Doris Langley Moore, Horace Annesley Vachell, Ernest Oldmeadow, J. B. Morton, Osbert Sitwell, all appear in the issues of these years. But the most regular contributor was André L. Simon himself. He wrote, of course, all the editorials, and reading through them one can trace the development of his ideas and what had become the principal aim of his life, the enhancement of gastronomic knowledge in Great Britain. But these were not the only products of his pen. There were many articles signed with his name or with his initials, A.L.S., the titles of which show the drift of his thought and his interests. 'Californian Wines', 'Bordeaux Vintages and Châteaux', 'Cognac Brandy', 'Alsace and its Wines', 'The London Docks Wine Vaults', 'The Wines of Burgundy', 'A Great Wine Auction', 'New York and Boston Revisited', 'An American Hotel

Wine List', make up a fair selection. He also wrote up, together with A. J. A. Symons and others, descriptions of 'Memorable Meals'.

Wine and Food was an important publication, accepted as it was as the prime organ of gastronomy in England. Its influence extended far beyond the restricted circles of the Wine and Food Society. And it reflected the personality of its editor.

André's prestige was undimmed. The gastronomic revolution was proceeding apace, and his position as its leader was hardly questioned. As a writer on wine only Warner Allen could rival him; and though Allen's knowledge was profound few would have disputed that André was the finer, and certainly the more readable, writer.

Physically he was developing into the majestic and impressive figure that so many of us remember. He had put on considerable weight; hardly surprising in view of all those memorable meals. He had always been substantial; one member of his family has told me that he weighed fifteen stone at the time of his marriage. This seems hard to believe; he certainly does not look it in the post-wedding photo of 1900. But in his later years – he was approaching sixty now – his rotundity was the most conspicuous feature of his make-up. It added greatly to the impressive benignity of his appearance.

He continued to write books, in addition to his contributions to his own magazine; but many of his productions now were of an ephemeral, not to say trivial, nature. He produced *A Catechism concerning Cheeses* and, a little surprisingly, a book on German wines. But such efforts as these had little impact; nor were they destined to rank among his memorabilia.

He was planning, however, in the peaceful seclusion of his office at Mather and Crowther's, a more ambitious venture, which was to be his most substantial work since the *History of the Wine Trade in England.* This was conceived as *A Concise Encyclopaedia of Gastronomy*, a compendium which would embrace the whole compass of the motivation that was now closest to his heart.

It was a big undertaking, but André, once he had thought out his project, proceeded with his usual determination. The first section, *Sauces*, was soon ready, and was actually published in the early months of 1939. By this time the second section, *Fish*, had also been written, but publication had to be postponed, though not for long, when war broke out.

André's reputation as a judge of wine was established and unassailable. Many are the stories told of those who can, by mere taste and smell, pronounce on the brand and the vintage of a particular wine. Those who can really do so are very few and far between; outside the closed ranks of the wine trade they are almost non-existent. André was certainly one of them. His enormous experience and the extreme sensitivity of his palate made him virtually infallible. Many of his old friends have borne witness to his expertise in this regard. A story is told of him which probably relates to this period of the 1930s.

A group of wine merchants, it is said, decided to test his capacity; he was given a succession of glasses of different wines, and he was asked to say, literally blindfold, what each wine was. He sampled each one in turn, and after a moment's reflection he named the wine and the vintage. Finally his hosts offered him, still blindfold, a glass of plain water. This gave him pause. He rolled it round the glass, sniffed, and tasted. At length he gave his verdict.

'I don't know what it is,' he said solemnly. 'I doubt if I ever tasted it before. But I can tell you one thing. It won't sell.'

Among his many friends he was as popular as ever. His gaiety and vitality broke down all barriers; he was the life and soul

of innumerable convivial assemblies. But he was much saddened by the death of one of his closest and most valued
companions.

André's senior by a year, Francis Lawrence Berry, of the
famous and venerable wine firm of Berry Brothers, was only
fifty-nine when he died suddenly on 2 March 1936. In a
generous tribute to his memory André wrote in the summer
number of *Wine and Food*:

Francis Berry, a shrewd business man with a wonderful
artistic sense, was as completely free from being grasping
or mean, which spoils the character of so many successful
business men, as he was free from the conceit which
renders ridiculous or unbearable some of the most gifted
artists.

The catholicity and intensity of his sense of appreciation
were extraordinary. He must have been often pained, but
he was never bored; he was sometimes irritable, but never
indifferent . . . He was irresistibly attracted by all that was
rare and beautiful, by all that was really good and genuine,
and he loathed and detested all fakes and misfits. He was
impulsive, quick-witted and quick-tempered, and both
his wit and temper had a sharp edge which made him
either the most entertaining of companions or the most
difficult, but he was always perfectly natural: he never
tried to be amusing, nor did he ever mean to hurt anybody's feelings; he was just himself, spontaneously and
genuinely enthusiastic or disgusted as the case might be
. . . He was the most admirable host imaginable, giving
his guests the finest wines perfectly matched as to the food
which was served with them, and in the finest possible
glasses, and giving them also more than a mere impression, a sort of conviction that he was happy in their
company. He had a very sure and very cultured taste in
wine and food, as well as in most forms of art. He was also a

very keen gardener. Above all, he was most generous; he did his utmost never to let it be known, but the number of lame dogs whom he helped unobtrusively over difficult stiles was very large indeed. Francis Berry was the prototype of what a connoisseur should be: artistic by disposition, painstaking and accurate by training, he had acquired a thorough knowledge of every branch of art which he had made his hobby, and he was ever ready gladly to share with his many friends his knowledge, his doubts and his joys. To me, and to many more, he was far more than a man of taste and wit: he was a true friend and a very dear one.

Berry was a sad loss. And his death was followed a year later by that of Professor Henry Armstrong, who had been one of the early pillars of the Wine and Food Society and had since been a regular contributor to *Wine and Food*. But there were still old friends with whom André could share good food and good wine. Ian Campbell, his other old crony of long standing, was still a good companion. Another of the old brigade was Horace Annesley Vachell, novelist and wine-lover. Vachell and his brother Arthur had bought a beautiful house, Widcombe Manor near Bath, and there André was always welcome.

· 'It has been my privilege', wrote Vachell in his autobiography, *Distant Fields*, 'to drink wine with our high priests of Bacchus: my generous guide, the late Francis Berry, uncrowned king of wine merchants; my old schoolfellow, John Martin Harvey of Bristol, whose memory is ever green; André Simon, an incomparable host; Colonel Ian Campbell, and many others.'

It was in these years that the dispersion of the Simon family was completed. André and Edith saw little of Jeanne at this time. She had a young son now, and she and her husband spent much of their time on the Continent.

André the younger was also away from the parental home. He had married his first wife at the end of 1931, and he too had a son; he had set up for himself as an independent wine merchant in London.

Peter was in the midst of the long and arduous Jesuit noviciate. He had moved from Manresa to Heythrop College, at Chipping Norton in Oxfordshire, and there André visited him from time to time. Father Peter Simon has a vivid recollection of one such visit:

We were about 150 in community (one year 153, the number of fish in the miraculous draught) and among us was a Jesuit Lay Brother with a flair for experimenting in the Lord's – and his own – vineyard. In the greenhouses was a flourishing vine, which the vine-dresser kept trimmed. Our Lay Brother, looking at the clusters lying on the ground and about to be swept away to the compost heap, thought – what a waste! So he gathered up all the clusters of small, raw grapes and carried them off to his cellar. After pressing, etc., he was ready for a tasting. Would A.L.S. oblige? Of course he would. Knowing nothing of the history of this bottled sunshine he sipped as he'd often sipped before and straightway spat as he'd never spat before!

The next to leave home was Madeleine, the youngest of the family. It had not been decided what she was going to do in life, but she provided the answer herself. She had always been devoted to her religion, and now became certain of her vocation; she was going to be a nun. She entered the noviciate of the Society of the Sacred Heart at the age of twenty on 22 October 1932. The Society of the Sacred Heart was at that time an enclosed community, though its rule was destined to be relaxed in this respect in the years to come.

The only one of André and Edith's children remaining was

thus Marcelle – and this not for very long. She too had long felt the call of the religious life, but she had stayed at home to be a companion for her mother. Now she felt that the call could no longer be ignored, and she yearned to follow the example of her younger sister. Her choice was the strictly enclosed Order of Discalced Carmelites, and she took the Carmelite habit in 1935.

Marcelle was a true Simon. Being asked by her father what treat she would like for her last night in the secular world, she chose an epicurean dinner at the Savoy.

Her parents were naturally distressed at losing the last of their children, one whom henceforth they would see only occasionally, and then in accordance with the strictest convent restrictions. But they were the last people to resist the call of religious duty. A letter survives from a friend and neighbour which gives expression to the feelings aroused:

> 23, Carlisle Mansions,
> Carlisle Place,
> Westminster, S.W.1.
> 26th August, 1935.

Dear Monsieur Simon,

Many thanks for your kind letter . . .

I read your letter with great sadness, for I know well what the disappearance of Marcelle from your life must mean to you and Madame Simon. I think anyone whose son or daughter takes to the religious life must always be torn in two between the glory of the spiritual venture and the mundane sadness of missing the bodily presence. I do sympathise with you both very much. I shall often think of Marcelle in her Carmelite robes and shall be glad and proud to think that I once knew her.

> Yours very sincerely,
> Gladys Scott Thomson

Marcelle was nearly thirty-three, a comparatively late age for taking the veil; friends were not lacking who prophesied that she would not stay the course. Today Sister Marcelle of Jesus is in her eighties; she has been twice prioress of her convent in Yorkshire, and has also served as mistress of novices. There is nothing to suggest that she has ever regretted the decision she made in 1935.

André and Edith Simon were left alone in Evelyn Mansions and at Little Hedgecourt. Fortunately they were ideally satisfied with each other's company.

Wartime Pause

THE dispersal of the Simon family caused André and Edith to reflect on their country home, Little Hedgecourt. It had, they came to the conclusion, outlived its usefulness. They loved it, but they had visualised an old age there with grandchildren, and perhaps great-grandchildren, coming and going in the summer months, 'boys and girls who would play tennis, bowls or cricket, act their own plays or charades, practise approach shots, niblick shots and long putts on a well-guarded green'. The dreams had faded. Of their children Jeanne and André were married with one son each; but they had their own lives to lead and were seldom at Little Hedgecourt. The other three had all dedicated themselves to the religious life, and would come no more to the parental home.

And so, in the summer of 1939, they decided to sell the house. It would be a wrench, but it was no longer worth the expense of keeping up; 'the lawns immediately in front and at the back of the house were kept in order', wrote André later, 'but as soon as one wandered further afield there was naught but depressing sights, the hard-tennis court sheer desolation, the open-air theatre a wilderness, the bowling green completely moss-eaten.' The approach of war, which overshadowed all else at that time, made the hope of enjoying country life even more remote.

So Little Hedgecourt went on the market. A sum of £8,000 was asked, which was about half what the Simons had paid for the house and estate in 1919; a considerable amount had been spent on it since then. A prospective buyer was quickly found, willing to pay the price demanded with no reductions. All seemed to be in train when it occurred to André to ask his agent who the buyer was. He was told that he was a builder who intended to construct a row of houses, from road to lake, after bulldozing the stretches of rhododendrons and azaleas that André had so lovingly tended through the years.

This was too much for the proprietor of Little Hedgecourt. It might be no concern of his what happened when the place was no longer his; but reason hardly entered into the matter. All his gardener's instincts rebelled. He just could not bear to think of all the beauty he had created being ruthlessly destroyed in favour of bricks and mortar; whatever the financial implications, it just would not do. So he instructed the agent to ask for another £2,000, which he was sure the potential client would not agree to pay. So it turned out. There was some unrealistic haggling, and eventually the client offered £1,000. Then came the war, and the whole deal was called off.

Little Hedgecourt remained a possession of the Simon family until many years after André's death.

In World War I André Simon had played an active, indeed a gallant part; serving in arms and performing valuable service for both France and Britain. World War II was different. He was in his sixties now, and it did not appear that there was any practical way in which he could make a direct contribution to the war effort. It seemed to him that the best course would be to continue his work of keeping gastronomic progress going, and so help the cause of civilisation in the peace that must eventually follow hostilities. In other words he would see that good living was not completely obliterated by austerity and rationing, and that there would be a foundation to build on when the evil times were over.

In any case, events forced his hand. It soon became apparent that, if the Wine and Food Society was to survive in any shape or form, thus furthering André's gastronomic designs, he would have to give all his time to it.

Rationing came in with the outbreak of hostilities, and its advent gave A. J. A. Symons a brainwave. Why should not the Wine and Food Society bring out a parody of the official ration book issued to all and sundry, a parody which would at the same time give an indication of ways in which good food and good liquor might still be enjoyed without infringing the ration laws?

The idea might not seem one of startling originality; but it filled A.J. with all the enthusiasm of his fervent nature. He was convinced that the parody would sell to the extent of anything up to a million copies, and would incidentally make a fortune for himself. The work was set in hand immediately.

The Unration Book duly appeared. It was similar in size and shape to the official book, the colour being blue instead of beige. The coupons, which were never to be cut off, had numbers, and each one corresponded with a food or dish which could be procured without difficulty – mostly fish, vegetables, game and fruit. At the end was a long list of unrationed foods, compiled by André. 'It was no cookery book, of course,' he wrote of the work, 'but it did remind you that a herring, for instance, could be boiled, fried, grilled, baked, soused, etc., each sort having a coupon number of its own.'

As a parody *The Unration Book* still has the power to amuse. Its title reads: 'The Unration Book which has nothing whatsoever to do with any Government, and is based solely on common sense'; and it is further announced: 'This book is transferable. It may be used by the consumer whose name is on the cover or by anybody else.' As an example of its version of wartime officialese the following, under 'Notes on Beer, Wines and Spirits', may be quoted:

Sizes of bottles.

Owing to wartime restrictions, wines are now available only in bottles of the following sizes: the nip, or quarter bottle; the half bottle; the imperial pint; the bottle; the magnum, or double bottle; the tregnum, or triple bottle; the jeroboam or double magnum; and the tuppit-hen, which equals half a cock. Consumers requiring wines in other sizes should apply to the nearest Food Restriction office, stating the purpose to which they propose putting the wine when obtained.

The Unration Book served its purpose in creating a certain amount of laughter in the war's early stages, and was reasonably successful. A.J.'s sanguine forecast of the sale of a million copies, however, was wildly astray. One obstacle of which he had taken no account was the paper shortage, which made itself felt as soon as war broke out. The printing of anything like a million copies was far beyond the bounds of possibility.

As to the Government, the parody was not likely to appeal to the humourless mind of officialdom. No action, however, was taken; there was really none that could be. It is believed, however, that it was privately indicated to the president of the Wine and Food Society that the venture was not considered to be conducive to the war effort.

The actual authorship of *The Unration Book* has never been conclusively established. It was issued anonymously, and was perhaps a joint production. But the main author was almost certainly Symons. It does not figure in André's very full lists of his own works in *By Request* and *In the Twilight*. Julian Symons, biographer of A.J., considers that the humour displayed is more typical of his brother's style than of André's.

If it was indeed A.J.'s work, it was his swan song. Towards the end of 1939 he was taken suddenly ill with a malady the

nature of which remained for some time mysterious. Julian
Symons recounts what happened:

> One day in November A.J. was brought home to Cedars
> Road in a cab. It was obvious that he was alarmingly ill. He
> was unable to walk without assistance, he was hardly able
> to articulate, and he was afflicted by a paralysis which
> made it impossible for him to hold a cup in his hands
> without spilling its contents. He lay for two weeks in his
> great bedroom at Clapham, unable to bear light or
> warmth, or to take any food other than soup and gruel.
> Then, nursed devotedly by my mother, his condition
> slowly improved, although he did not recover fully. He
> hardly moved out of bed for weeks, and when he did get up
> his power of locomotion was uncertain. This distressed
> him less, however, than his inability to articulate clearly,
> and the need to rely on others to sign the letters which he
> dictated in a blurred and feeble voice.

Specialists were called in, but to little avail. For a time it
was believed that the illness was encephalitis, or sleeping
sickness. Whatever it was, it was obvious that he was quite
incapable of attending to any sort of business. After a time he
was moved to his country home at Finchingfield in Essex.

André was thus left in sole charge of the Wine and Food
Society. He had to do all the office work in addition to
arranging what functions he could to take his members'
minds off war and rationing. In the early stages he was more
successful in this latter aim than might have been thought
possible. There was little hope of enrolling new members,
and it was hardly the time for agitating for the payment of
subscriptions. But somehow the Society managed to keep
going. The blackout made dinners impossible, but luncheons were held and were surprisingly well attended. During
the first six months of hostilities (the 'phony war' period), as

recorded in *By Request*, 'we met for lunch at the Gargoyle
Club on 22 November, at the Waldorf Hotel on 6 December,
at the Dorchester on 20 December, at Oddenino's on 3 and 4
January, at the Carlton Hotel on 24 January, at the Langham
Hotel on 22 and 23 February, at the Park Lane Hotel on 5
March, and at the Connaught Rooms on 26 April.' This was a
sterling achievement, even though austere spirits might
regard it as falling short of the best way of fighting the war
against Hitler. To André at least it was all part of the
paramount task of preserving the standards of civilisation.

Moreover a 'Lucullus Group' had been formed of members who aimed at a higher gastronomic standard than the
Society as a whole; and this group found itself able to stage a
dinner at the Ritz on 17 January 1940, at which André was
invited to be the guest of honour. The menu gives an idea of
what it was found possible to serve at perhaps the last
function of its kind to be arranged in wartime:

Bêches de Mer au Sherry

Saumon braisé au Château de Nozet

Jaquette d'Agneau rôti
Velouté de Champignons
Pommes nouvelles

Terrine de Bécasse
Salade d'Escarole aux fines herbes

Soufflé Fribourgeoise

Café

The wines were worthy of the occasion, the clarets including
a Château Chalon 1919, a Château Petrus 1924, a Château
Haut-Brion 1923 and a Château Cheval Blanc 1900. There
was also André's 'own "Cuvée" of Pommery 1921, which

had been shipped to me in magnums only and as "Super-brut".' It was a memorable meal indeed.

All this sort of thing came to an abrupt end when the war ceased to be 'phony'. The fall of France, and the new phase that now came about, made it unthinkable that such institutions as the Wine and Food Society should continue to make merry. The Society was not disbanded, but it went into a state of suspended animation from which it was felt to be doubtful if it would ever emerge.

The collapse of France affected André deeply. Through all his happy years in England he had never ceased to be a patriotic Frenchman, and the thought of his beloved country under the heel of its hereditary foe was almost more than he could bear. On a lower scale the complete cessation of the import of French wines set the seal on the effective demise of the Wine and Food Society.

His distress was aggravated by a series of petty squabbles with Symons. André was finding his single-handed management of the Society's affairs irksome, and he was irritated to discover that its financial state left much to be desired. Symons was careless about money. He had himself overdrawn his share of the Society's profits, and had left a number of accounts unpaid. André felt that too much had been left to him to unravel, and he resented the fact that A.J., too ill to do his share of the work, was yet well enough to take a prolonged holiday in Cornwall.

This trouble did not last. The quarrel, such as it was, was smoothed over. But for a time a somewhat acrimonious correspondence was carried on between Little Hedgecourt and Finchingfield.

It is clear that at this time André was suffering from acute mental distress. He was in an uncharacteristically nervous state; he was unable to concentrate on essentials, and all activities were a burden to him. It is equally clear that he had little idea of how serious his partner's illness really was.

A. J. A. Symons died at Finchingfield on 26 August 1941. His malady was finally diagnosed as a haemangioma of the brain stem, a complaint that involves a brain haemorrhage. He was forty-one years old.

'We who knew him best mourn him most,' wrote André in the autumn number of *Wine and Food*, 'but he will be greatly missed by all. His place can never be filled: there will never be anybody like him. We have seen many young lives lost in air battles and air raids during the past year, but the tragedy of A.J.'s death cannot be gauged by any measure of mourning or heartache. It has removed from a world gravely menaced by the rising tide of mediocrity and vulgarity a man of exquisite taste and brilliant intellect, of many gifts and outstanding personality, one who had mastered in an incredibly short span of years a complete command of hand, fount and speech – Calligraphy, Typography, and Oratory.'

The war did not make very much difference to André's mode of existence. His domestic life, which was what mattered most to him now, was as happy and tranquil as ever. At the beginning of the war Jeanne, with her husband and their son Emile, left Switzerland just in time to get their car across the Channel, and made for Little Hedgecourt, where André and Edith were only too glad to accommodate them. William Rouyer Guillet had been rejected on medical grounds for service with the French Army, and he was now similarly rejected when he tried to join the British forces.

Any acrimony which may have lingered on from the events of 1932–3 was blown away by the gusts of war. Jeanne and William were to make Little Hedgecourt their home for many years to come, and André from now on was as close to his favourite daughter as he had been in the days before her marriage.

The Simons settled down to country life. The flat in

Evelyn Mansions was for the time given up, and was requisitioned by the Government. So Little Hedgecourt became their only home, and after the collapse and death of A. J. A. Symons it also became the official address of the Wine and Food Society.

It was a crowded house. André had given a home to a London family with five young children, and these evacuees stayed for the duration. The estate too caused its troubles. East Grinstead was on the direct route to London used by German bombers. 'There were anti-aircraft batteries close to us,' André wrote; 'whether they ever shot down an enemy plane we do not know, but we could tell that they never were short of ammunition. It also happened on rare occasions that the German airmen did not like the look of things ahead and decided to go home, but before doing so they let go their load of bombs haphazard; rightly or wrongly, that was the best way we had thought of to account for bombs on such unmilitary targets as our garden, uncomfortably close to the house.'

War Ministry officials discovered that the lake at the end of the garden was a guide-line to the German pilots; so it had to be drained. But it was found that the stream through the middle could still be seen from the air; the solution now devised was to stick in quantities of young trees that André had allowed the authorities to cut down in the garden.

If André felt that there was nothing very much he could do in direct furtherance of the war effort, he could at least take pride in the exploits of the next generation. For André *fils* had a highly creditable war record.

Like his sister Jeanne, the younger André was on the Continent in September 1939. But unlike her he had no race with time to get to the shores of England. Holding dual nationality, he stayed in France and joined the French Army. In the brief campaign that followed the German invasion he was taken prisoner, but he soon escaped, and it was only then that he entered on the hazardous venture of getting to England. It took him two years. He made contact with the French Resistance fighters, with whom henceforth he was to be associated, and with their help he eventually made his way through occupied France, and then through Spain, getting across the Channel in 1941.

Like his father in the earlier conflict, André *fils* would never talk about his war adventures, except in the form of light-hearted accounts of some of his escapades. But in fact he performed valuable services. He joined Special Operations Executive, the celebrated SOE which maintained liaison with the French Resistance. After parachute training he was dropped many times into France, sometimes for the purpose of helping a French leader to get from one country to the other, but mostly to help the Maquis with arms and personnel. He was awarded the MBE – recognition which many of his friends thought inadequate – by the British, and the Croix de Guerre by the French. In the last months of the war he was a member of Duff Cooper's Embassy in Paris.

André *père* was able, rather surprisingly, to pay one final visit to his own country after war was declared. In April 1940 he flew to Paris, and from there went by train to Dreux, where he was met by Pierre, youngest of the Simon brothers. Pierre, all his life a farmer, drove him out to his farm, where Mme Ernest Simon was still living; thus André was able to see his aged mother for the last time. This was the prime object of his journey, and having said goodbye to her he returned to Paris by rail and to London by air.

For the rest of the war years he lived quietly at Little Hedgecourt, though with frequent visits to London. He found plenty to occupy his time, and his passion for gardening increased. He had a full household to look after, and the constant passing of German planes ensured that the nights should not be boring.

The London visits were mainly devoted to the production of *Wine and Food*. The Wine and Food Society itself was dormant, but its magazine still came out. André's energy and enthusiasm were undimmed, and he was anxious to show that the Society was still alive by seeing that its members continued to receive its journal regularly. From beginning to end of the war no number failed to appear.

This was no mean achievement. André did all the office work, and at times the task appeared insuperable. The worst headache was the paper shortage, and more than once it appeared that there would not be enough for the next issue. But the Curwen Press of Plaistow, who printed *Wine and Food*, rallied round splendidly. They were, as André recorded, 'located in one of the most heavily bombed areas of Greater London, but they never ran away and never shut down; when they were hit, they picked themselves up and carried on; and when they could not print *Wine and Food* on the due date, they got it printed by some other firm for them.' The moving spirit of the Curwen Press was Oliver Simon (the name Simon again), who proved a true friend in time of trouble, going to endless pains to procure the necessary supplies of paper. The fact that the American members of the Society loyally kept up their subscriptions throughout the war also played an important part in securing the paper.

Another friend, Ben McPeake of the National Magazine Company, was likewise useful. He was a member of the Wine and Food Society, and when he read in *Wine and Food* of the death of A. J. A. Symons he made an offer to André. His firm carried on its publishing activities in Grosvenor Gardens, and with its depleted staff it had room to spare. Would André like to use an office in Grosvenor Gardens?

André accepted the suggestion with alacrity; once more he had an office in London, and from then on the business of producing *Wine and Food* became altogether easier. More-over McPeake also offered the services of his distributing organisation to handle the Society's publications. It was a great boon. 'This was, I consider,' we read in *By Request*, 'the turning point in the affairs of the Wine and Food Society: it placed its publishing upon a sound and profitable basis which set my mind free from that day to this from financial anxieties.'

A glance at the wartime issues of *Wine and Food* shows how well the standard was maintained. The size of the magazine had to be cut down, and the paper shortage caused its appearance to vary a little; but the efforts of Oliver Simon bore fruit, and the journal appears different from the peace-time issues only when closely perused. The old contributors loyally continued their support. The names of Ian Campbell, Sir Francis Colchester-Wemyss, Sir Stephen Gaselee, Maurice Healy, Jack Drummond and James Laver con-tinued to grace the pages of *Wine and Food*. Ernest Old-meadow was a constant standby. In 1941 he began a series of articles entitled *Ration-cum-Reason Recipes*, which gave valuable and practical advice on how to enjoy good food under wartime restrictions. 'Mr Ernest Oldmeadow', wrote André in the editorial of the spring number, '. . . has long made a hobby of frugal yet not uninteresting cookery . . . He addresses himself to the amateur, as an amateur cook himself of no mean merit, one who is thrice blessed since he possesses a sensitive palate, a keen sense of humour, and the gift of expression. He has chosen for his text *appetitus rationi abediant*, "Let appetites obey reason", and he means us, no doubt, to obey *rationibus*, in Lord Woolton's sense, as well as *ratio*, in Cicero's.'

As always, the most regular contributor was André him-self. He wrote happily on all aspects of gastronomy, giving hope of better times to come. In the first wartime issue there was an article from his pen on the 1939 vintage in France, the last vintage that England could hope to see for some time. In the next he wrote on 'Wine and Tobacco', discussing the circumstances in which the two might go together. Unlike some other wine-lovers, André did not consider that smoking necessarily ruined the palate, and he was a living witness to the contrary. All through his life he was a cigar-smoker.

When he felt that his own name was appearing too much in *Wine and Food*, he would write under a pseudonym, always retaining the sacred initials A.L.S. Such names as Albert L. Savage, who contributed some 'Notes on Rice' to the spring number of 1941, quickly revealed the authorship to those in the know.

Death continued to be busy with André's old cronies. A loss he felt deeply was that of Maurice Healy, KC, his beloved pupil, who died on 9 May 1943 at the early age of fifty-five. Intimacy between the two had grown with the years, and the obituary article written by André was perhaps the most eloquent of all such tributes which he contributed to *Wine and Food*. He spoke of Healy's sensitive taste, his keen ear for music and for words, his wit, his gifts as a host, his charity and religious devotion, his literary work for the cause of good wine which he 'offered to a delighted and ever-increasing public in the form of a new wine wisdom'. He told the story of their long friendship, and he ended with the sentence with which he began: 'Peace has now come to him and grief to all who knew him, for none ever knew him who did not love him.'

Less than three years earlier André had reviewed Maurice's last and best-known book, *Stay Me with Flagons*, a happy tribute to wine which took its place among the elder man's favourite reading matter. 'All his readers are his friends', he then wrote, 'and he is, in this latest book of his, their host. He is not soliloquizing nor preaching, but just chatting to them all in these delightful pages, as the most gifted of conversationalists, imparting knowledge and dispensing entertainment at the same time.'

Later in the year came the deaths of two more old friends – Sir Stephen Gaselee, a comrade of long standing, and the incomparable restaurateur Marcel Boulestin. André, to whom the companionship of old friends was one of the greatest joys of existence, felt all these losses deeply.

Apart from *Wine and Food*, André's principal interest in these years of war was the completion of his *Concise Encyclopaedia of Gastronomy*. Into this he put his heart and soul. It was his most ambitious literary work for many years; there were seven sections still to go, and he was determined to get them finished. He spent many hours at the Natural History Museum, 'looking through a very large number of books for reliable and entertaining data about all the edible birds, beasts, fruits or plants which were to be found in different parts of the world, and for trustworthy records of when and how and by whom they had been eaten'. The work took him beyond the end of the war, but in 1946 the last of the nine sections was printed. They were published as they came out by the Wine and Food Society, and printed once more by the invaluable Curwen Press. Procuring the necessary paper was still a great headache, but Oliver Simon achieved it with the indefatigable help of André himself, who 'started hunting in highways and by-ways for odds and ends of paper supplies in the hands of out-of-the-way small printers or others'.

It was his last wartime labour of love, though not destined for a number of years yet to come out as a complete single volume. It certainly ranks as one of his major compilations.

So the years passed busily. Before the end André decided that the Wine and Food Society need no longer lie dormant. In 1941 the members had been told that 'the next dinner will be our Victory Dinner; its date will be announced later.'

Dinners were not yet possible, but after the Normandy landings, when ultimate victory became inevitable, André resolved that a victory lunch could be held. He went to the Connaught Rooms and booked the Great Hall for a luncheon, which would be followed by the annual general meeting of the Society on Monday, 16 October 1944.

Gastronome in Chief

THE luncheon duly took place on the planned date, 16 October 1944. It was a success as an augury for the future, whatever its intrinsic merits or demerits. Even André with his sanguine outlook came to the conclusion that it would be premature to proclaim it a victory meal; in his speech as chairman he announced that 'our meeting today is not our Victory Meeting – not yet.' It was a memorable occasion none the less; the Wine and Food Society emerged from its long wartime sleep, and the function marked the eleventh anniversary of the foundation of the Society.

It was not, of course, a meal that for quality could be compared with the more memorable repasts of pre-war years. The five-shilling limit for one main course and two subsidiaries was still in force, and to procure wines of distinction in the bulk necessary was impossible. But more than three hundred members and guests (mostly guests) turned up at the Connaught Rooms, and André's friend Sir Jack Drummond, now scientific adviser to the Ministry of Food, arranged for the Minister, Colonel J. J. Llewellin, to be present.

The fare was simple, and André later described it as 'the worst meal we ever had'; the menu announced 'Scallops Connaught; Roast Partridge Bonne Femme; Braised Cabbage and Potatoes Annette; Apple and Sultana Pudding.' With the fish there was an Alsatian Sylvaner, which was followed by an Algerian red, described by André as 'sound enough and acceptable'. After years of rationing and austerity, it all seemed a worthy reward.

André in his speech paid generous tribute to the work done in the difficult years by the Ministry of Food, and voiced hopes for the future. And the Minister, in his reply, showed that at least there was some appreciation in government circles of what André and the Society were trying to do, of the campaign that could now be renewed to improve the quality of good living in Britain. Colonel Llewellin said:

> There are some clever caterers who use flavours and sauces to disguise bad and worthless food. Others use them to enhance still further the flavour of good food.
>
> If your society can do anything to encourage the latter and to discourage the former it will deserve well of this nation. You could also do more even than in the past to deal with the problems of our country inns and hotels, not only by advising us which ones to go to, but by giving advice to proprietors, chefs, and cooks how to prepare good food and how to serve good wines.
>
> We hope that after the war people will come here from abroad to visit us – Americans who have been serving here and their relatives, and refugees who have already spent some years among us. Let us see that there are good houses and hotels and inns in which they can stay.
>
> Let us see to it if we can, too, that we have places such as you can find in every little country town and village in France, where you can get a first-class *dejeuner*. That is what we should aim at in our small towns and villages throughout Britain – places where you can get attractive food and attractive wines as well.

It was all very encouraging, and André felt that the revived Wine and Food Society had got off to a good start. His next move was to improve on the Connaught Rooms lunch. This was in itself not difficult. Among his guests at that function was an old friend, Barry Neame of the Hind's Head Hotel at Bray-on-Thames, always renowned for its good food. Neame had been contemptuous of the meal, pronouncing the 'partridges' to be seagulls; but he now undertook to provide a lunch at the Hind's Head on two different days 'that would be a surprise and a joy to any pernickety gastronome'. The price would be the same as at the Connaught Rooms, thirty shillings a head: 5s. for three courses, 25s. for wines and service.

Neame stipulated that at each of the duplicated luncheons there should be an attendance of no more than fifty: the function was therefore limited to members of the Society; no guests, and no invitations to the press. There was a reason for this. Neame had just two imperials of Château Lascombes 1929, a great claret now at its best, and he proposed to bring out one of these at each of the luncheons. An imperial, the largest of the giant wine measures occasionally bottled, will serve fifty drinkers but no more.

This was the gem of the feast, which took place on 14 and 15 November 1944. There was also a superb white burgundy, a Bâtard Montrachet of the same year as the claret. As for the food, 'we started', says André's account, 'with an excellent piping hot soup of fresh vegetables and ended with treacle tart, but the main dish was pheasants that were exactly right, tender, moist, tasty, hung just long enough, not high, quite perfect, and as much as you cared to ask for. Not bad for the legal five shillings.'

Both functions went splendidly. André was enchanted, and so were the limited number of lunchers privileged to be present. Not for the first or last time, Barry Neame had proved a valuable friend to the Wine and Food Society and its president.

All was now well. The Society was well and truly re-launched, and André could look forward to organising an unlimited series of gastronomic functions on the old model. In point of fact it was not attempted to put on any more meals while the war in Europe continued, but after VE Day the programme was resumed.

Once again the Connaught Rooms were booked – for another lunch which was held on Empire Day, 24 May 1945. It was very much an imperial occasion. The High Commissioner for Australia, S. M. Bruce, was in the chair, and he was supported by the corresponding officials for Canada, New Zealand and South Africa. All the wines served were Australian or South African.

This was classed as the ninety-second meeting of the Wine and Food Society; the first Connaught Rooms lunch had been the ninetieth. There were to be no more long gaps. The Society moved steadily forward towards its century of 'meetings'.

There was a great boon both to André and to the Society at this time. This was none other than a first-rate replacement for A. J. A. Symons. With the renewal of activities there was a great need of a secretary. André, keeping up his office in Grosvenor Gardens, was running the Society single-handed; but the burden of all the office work, in addition to thinking out and organising the functions, was too much for him to take on. Assistance had to be found.

The first to take office was Robin Adair, who had been one of the earliest members of the Wine and Food Society. André offered him the post of secretary as from June 1945, with three months' holiday to begin with. The holiday was necessary. Adair had been a prisoner in occupied France, and his experiences in a German concentration camp had badly affected his health and his nerves. So it was that the first meeting of the Society to which he had to attend was also the last. This was another lunch at the Connaught Rooms, once more on 16 October, with the annual general meeting to follow. It duly took place, and all seemed well. But it was too much for Robin Adair. He was taken seriously ill soon after the luncheon, and was advised by his doctor not to spend another winter in London. He resigned the post and went to live in Ireland.

It was a blow after what had seemed to be an ideal arrangement, but Adair performed a last and valuable service to the Society. It was through his good offices that another replacement was found. Her name was Marjorie Fletcher.

Miss Fletcher entered on her duties with calm and confident efficiency. The first function with which she had to deal was the real 'Victory Dinner', which at last took place at the Dorchester Hotel on 8 May 1946, the anniversary of VE Day. It was a great success. Sir Ben Smith, the new Minister of Food, was the chief guest, and among the others was A. P. Herbert, who had written a special grace and toast for the occasion. This he recited amid much enthusiasm:

> Thank God that we survive to see
> Our glasses full, our people free.
> Wherever friends and freedom dwell,
> We join their joy, and wish them well.
> For all the sick, the sad, the dead,
> Forget the glass and bow the head.
> Then lift your hearts and glasses high,
> For love and laughter shall not die.
> May the strong sun of Heaven shine
> In gracious men and golden wine.

Champagne was served throughout the meal. 'The room was full to capacity,' wrote André on the function, 'but the seating arrangements and the table plan were such that there was no confusion nor were there any complaints: I knew from that moment that I had drawn a winner in Marjorie Fletcher.'

This he had certainly done. Those who knew the Wine and Food Society in the days of Marjorie Fletcher's secretaryship recall her enthusiasm, her competence; the manner in which she identified herself with the Society and its doings. She made herself an expert in gastronomy, joined the president in organising the meetings, and became as much a part of the proceedings as was André himself. At the same time she became one of his closest and most valued friends.

Her advent gave André more freedom of movement than he had enjoyed for years, and he was able to devote himself to the wider aspects of his interests. The Society had expanded considerably, with branches extending throughout Britain and abroad. These new branches had been growing since the early days. Brighton and Liverpool had been the first. Now they existed in most of the larger cities; in addition there were branches in Melbourne and other big towns in Australia. The American chapters were flourishing.

During these post-war years André travelled the length and breadth of England, Wales, Scotland and Ireland, visiting the branches which his disciples had founded and developed. In the intervals he toured the vineyards of Bordeaux, Champagne and Alsace, with one or two visits thrown in to Spain and Switzerland. And in 1946 and 1948 he found time to resume his trips to America.

The 1946 visit marked the first occasion on which he had crossed the Atlantic by air. In six weeks he revisited New York, Boston, Chicago, San Francisco, Los Angeles and New Orleans, and went for the first time to Detroit, Milwaukee, Cincinnati, Kansas City and Baltimore, where new chapters of the Wine and Food Society were springing up. A new wave of gastronomic enthusiasm was manifest with the coming of peace. André was highly gratified with what he found in the New World.

He had resumed the old life with vigour. No. 6 Evelyn Mansions was de-requisitioned at the end of the war, and he and Edith once more spent most of their time in London. Jeanne was left in possession of Little Hedgecourt, where her parents were always her most welcome guests at weekends. And there André showed himself as ardent a gardener as ever.

All this culminated in the great event of 1950 – the golden wedding of André and Edith Simon. This was celebrated on 17 October, fiftieth anniversary of their marriage in London. Peter Simon, now a Jesuit priest, said Mass for his parents at 8 a.m. in the Lady Chapel of Westminster Cathedral, and had lunch with them at Evelyn Mansions before returning to Mount St Mary College in Yorkshire. In the evening André and Edith were the guests of honour at a Wine and Food Society dinner at the Dorchester, described by André as 'the most memorable meal of our lives'. Jeanne and André *fils* were there, and so was Ian Campbell, oldest of old friends. And there was an abundance of newer friends in the world of wine – George Rainbird, Leslie and Philip Hardern, Ronald Avery, the Dowager Lady Swaythling, Elizabeth Craig, Jack Drummond, Vyvyan Holland, and of course Marjorie Fletcher. René Massigli, the French Ambassador, was in the chair.

The splendid function can be adequately described only in André's own words:

. . . The room was magnificently dressed, with fifty round tables ablaze with tall wax candles and flowers and a wealth of glittering crystal glasses, five to each diner, two thousand nine hundred and thirty wine glasses, statisticians please note! The top table was festooned with golden chiffon, whilst a host of candles in four great silver-gilt candelabra shed their beams upon gold plate.

The dinner itself was not the usual banquet fare of soup,

sole, chicken and ice cream. The first two courses were cold, easily served and perfect in quality, Scotch smoked Salmon and Foie Gras in Aspic. Then came the main course, the only one to be hot, Roast Pheasant with Game Chips, and the usual trimmings. The sweet was an excellent Apple Pie with lashings of fresh Devonshire cream, by special permission of the Ministry of Food. Then came the Wedding Cake with its fifty lighted little candles. It was a truly wonderful confection by Fuller in the shape of an enormous 'open book' made of sponge cake, with a map of France in sugar on one side and a part of England on the other; painted in coloured fruits and sugar were the chief vineyards of France and, of course, my native village Paris. On the English side, there was Grantham well in evidence, being my wife's birthplace, and there was London, where we were married in 1900. Quite a work of art.

As to the wines, there was champagne in ample supply (Irroy) before dinner, then a cool glass of Poirier's 1946 Bâtard-Montrachet, which tasted very well indeed with the Foie Gras; there were two clarets escorting the pheasant, a 1943 Château Pichon-Longueville-Lalande, not a great wine but good and just right as a leader-up to the 1929 Château Haut-Bailly, the great wine of the evening. With the apple pie and the wedding cake, a chilled 1937 Château d'Yquem was refreshing and welcome; with the coffee we had a Cusenier 1900 Brandy.

My wife and I were presented each with a golden sovereign set in a little case with our initials, golden momentoes of a golden date.

. . . by far the greater number of our hosts on that memorable evening were men and women, some of whom we had known for a short time only, and others whom we knew not at all; yet they had all been sufficiently interested in us to want to come and meet us and rejoice with us. How grateful we were that we had made, in our old age, so many young friends!

A memorable occasion indeed.

This post-war period, it may be said, marked the climax of the gastronomic career of André Louis Simon. His position was unassailable. The whole outlook of Britain in matters of wine and food was changing. Before the war there had really been little interest in the finer points. There had of course been an inner circle of connoisseurs, but in general it had been taken for granted that English cookery was uninspired, while an appreciation of wine was best left to the French. From now on a new attitude to food and drink developed, an attitude emphasised by the emergence from years of wartime shortages. The average English man and woman began to take a genuine interest in the quality of what he or she ate or drank. Cookery was studied, and advantage taken of the example across the Channel. Restaurants flourished, and the reputation of English cooks emerged from the shadows. As for wine, Britain had always been renowned as a land of beer-drinkers. It would be too much to claim that there was any very profound change in this respect, but from 1945 onwards wine, imported once more from the Continent, appeared more and more on English tables and in the bars and restaurants of English hotels, inns and public houses. In the higher circles of wine-lovers there was genuine appreciation on a scale that had never been approached before.

Of this gastronomic revolution – and it was nothing less – André was the acknowledged leader; Frenchman though he was, he was Britain's leading gastronome. Perhaps only his old friend Herbert Warner Allen could claim to exercise anything approaching comparable influence; and Warner Allen, an erudite writer on wine, was an altogether more retiring figure, content to remain in the background and produce literary work for a limited public.

All who met André were impressed by his splendid presence. In his seventies now (he attained threescore and ten in 1947), he was white-headed and white-moustached, with those abundant crinkly locks that were so attractive. His portly figure and elegant bearing presented an appearance redolent alike of dignity and geniality.

It was in the mid-1950s that the present author made his acquaintance. The end of hostilities found me in the Far East. After war service in India and Burma I was demobilised in Singapore, and thereafter lived for ten years in Malaya. In Kuala Lumpur a few kindred spirits formed a branch of the Wine and Food Society; chief among them was the Chief Justice of Malaya, Sir Charles Mathew, who became the first chairman of the branch. I joined it soon after its formation, and this was my first direct connection with the Wine and Food Society.

In 1955 I returned to live once more in London, and in accordance with the rules took up membership of the parent Society. I was most hospitably received by Marjorie Fletcher, and from that time on became a regular attendant at the Society's 'meetings'. It did not take long to get on terms with the president. He received me, as he did all new members, with the utmost friendliness. I was a near neighbour of his in Pimlico, and our acquaintance had not developed far before I was invited to take a glass with him in Evelyn Mansions. There I met Madame Simon, who quickly attracted me with her vivacity and her friendliness.

It was André's appearance that first impressed me. He looked what he was, the very embodiment of good living and of good nature. The kind-heartedness that was his most abiding characteristic shone in his features.

I remember that quite early in our acquaintanceship I took one of my nieces, Brigid Utley, as my guest to one of the country lunches that were so pleasant a feature of the Wine and Food Society's programmes of those days. It was at the Bell at Aston Clinton, and when we arrived on a fine summer day at that delightful inn André was standing behind a table in the garden to receive the guests. He was immaculate in a light grey suit, the customary flower in his buttonhole; a more perfect example of a host could hardly be imagined. I presented my niece, who had not seen him before but of course knew all about him. As we left the table, Brigid delivered her verdict: 'André Simon looks exactly right.'

His energy and enthusiasm were as undimmed as was his conviviality. One of his oldest friends was H. A. Vachell, sixteen years his senior, who was to live, like André himself, to be a nonagenarian. Soon after the end of the war André was his guest at Widcombe Manor, and Vachell, in the journal which was the basis of his second volume of auto-biography, *Methuselah's Diary*, wrote of this 'too-brief visit': 'Again I write: "Que Dieu te garde, André!" His vitality would resurrect a corpse.' Vachell was now the president of the Bristol and Bath Wine and Food Society.

There were younger friends also. It was now that André came to know George Rainbird, who would one day take over from him as the leading light of the Wine and Food Society, a position he never lost. And as the 1950s wore on he became the friend and mentor of wine writers of a new generation, such as Cyril Ray and Hugh Johnson.

A friend who became particularly close was Joy Fontes, who was in main charge of the Cheshire branch of the Society. Mrs Fontes, now Mrs Arthur Rothwell, has many memories of the days of their friendship:

André Simon always replied to my letters (from Cheshire) by return of post, no matter how trifling were my ques-tions. He wrote in a lovely flowing longhand – later, when he was going blind, he taught himself to use a typewriter.

André never failed to give constructive criticism, in such a kindly fashion one felt privileged to receive it. One of his *bêtes noires* was being given any sort of wine in a small glass. He would smilingly tell the waiter 'I can't get my beeg nose into this,' and the offending article would be gladly replaced.

One of his better-known *bons mots* – when asked if he ever drank water, his invariable reply was, 'I'm told I have an iron constitution and I have no wish to rust it.'

As has been already remarked, it is said that André never learned to cook. Jeanne Rouyer Guillet bears this out. Mrs Rothwell, however, thinks this verdict should be modified. 'More than once,' she writes, 'when I was at his flat in Evelyn Mansions, he cooked an omelette for several of us, and, like any good cook should, insisted we went to the table at once.'

Another of Mrs Rothwell's memories:

At a dinner party there (Evelyn Mansions) one evening, when his old friend Alice Delysia was present, she was enjoying it all so much, she burst into song at the table. André, smiling, whispered to me, 'She wouldn't be singing if she realised there are thirteen of us at the table; she's very superstitious.'

André's principal interest, now as always, was the Wine and Food Society, which took on a new lease of life after the war. Membership increased, and the full programme of 'meetings' was fulfilled. Perhaps the standard was still not so high as in pre-war days. Economic conditions and the state of the wine trade made it difficult to arrange epicurean repasts at a reasonable price. The average member of the Society could not afford regular attendance at functions graced with the accompaniment of expensive vintages.

This said, there was plenty to afford satisfaction. Marjorie

Fletcher attended to the daily running of the Society's affairs, but it was André who arranged the meetings, devoting all his ingenuity to the organisation of new and enterprising ventures. He still had good friends in the wine trade, who were always ready to help.

A feature of this period was the inauguration of a series of one-day expeditions in the summer months to the vineyards and cellars of the great champagne houses – a series destined to be prolonged and expanded for many years. A plane or planes would be chartered, and the members flown to Rheims, there or at Epernay to be shown round the plant of one of the champagne firms; then came a tour of the vineyards, followed by lunch, with all the varieties of wine produced, in the cool of the cellars or in the sunshine at tables overlooking the Marne. Moët et Chandon, Ruinart, Irroy and others acted as hosts to the visitors. Many of us have the happiest of memories of those sun-filled days in the Valley of the Marne, with their frequent tastings of the best of good wine, and with André the benevolent despot of all the proceedings.

When it could be conveniently included, a détour would be made before the flight home to Hautvilliers, for a brief homage at the grave of Dom Pérignon.

Literary activities were resumed, partly in the form of revision. In 1951 *The Art of Good Living* was reissued, this time with a foreword by Sir Francis Meynell. Meanwhile the various sections of *A Concise Encyclopaedia of Gastronomy* had been produced, and in 1952 the complete *magnum opus* was published in a single volume by Collins.

The *Concise Encyclopaedia* is indeed concise; yet in this full edition it runs to nearly eight hundred pages. The nine sections are headed:

I   Sauces
II   Vegetables

Heralded as a book 'for the legion of gastronomes: those people blessed with all their senses and a sufficient willingness to use them, not abuse them, in the pursuit of a fuller and happier life', it is by any criterion a major work. Every aspect of gastronomy and the Good Life is covered. André never claimed to be a cook in the practical sense, but the precise instructions as to methods to be used in the preparation of dishes of every kind show that he had paid minute attention to the theory; he had studied thoroughly the art of cooking as revealed in the works and the work of the great chefs.

It would be hard to find a volume that covers the subject in more comprehensive detail. The *Concise Encyclopaedia* has maintained its relevance to the present day. There are connoisseurs of food and drink in the 1980s to whom *A Concise Encyclopaedia of Gastronomy* is the essential basis of all their knowledge and practice.

During the next few years books continued to appear, many of them published by the Wine and Food Society. Most of them are short and ephemeral, though useful, works of the kind that had always come fluently from André's pen. *Mushrooms Galore*, *The Gourmet's Week-End Book*, *How to Serve Wine in Hotels and Restaurants*, *How to Enjoy Wine in the Home*, *Wines and Liqueurs from A to Z*, *English Fare and French Wine*, *A Wine Primer* (a 'text-book for beginners on how to buy, keep and serve wine'), are titles that appear in the bibliographies for the early 1950s. Of more importance are *The Wine and Food Society Menu Book*, published in 1956, and *The Wines of France* in the following year. Then, in 1957, came the volume for which André's friends and admirers had long been waiting.

André had been in no hurry to write his memoirs. Now, pressed on all sides to do so, he felt the time had come. He was eighty years old and could look back on a full and happy life, the ups and downs of which were surely worth recording.

The Foreword to the book which appeared is worth giving in full, showing as it does how it came to be written and why the author entitled it *By Request*:

The world is made of all sorts, young and old, rich and poor, sick and fit, and so on.

What sort am I?

I will tell you.

But who cares?

Very few, but let me tell you.

There are now a great many members of the Wine and Food Society in all parts of the world: they all know the name of the President of the Society, who is also the editor of the Society's Quarterly, but most of them know absolutely nothing about him except that he is an old man who appears to enjoy still a remarkably fine appetite.

Why should they wish to know more?

I cannot tell, but I have been assured persistently and, at last, convincingly that they do.

Whether it be sheer inquisitiveness on their part, or real interest, I do not know, but I have been vain or foolish enough to agree to record as best as my memory would serve me the chief incidents, friendships and activities of my long life.

Hence this book of reminiscences published by the Wine and Food Society for its members.

Liberal quotations from *By Request* have appeared in the present work. It was, and remains, a delightful book, recording as it does the successes and failures, and portraying the personality, of a loved and lovable octogenarian, who had throughout the vicissitudes of life retained a sunny optimism, a deep love of God and a warm regard for his fellow men and women. We read of the early life in France with its background of Catholic royalism, of the first steps in journalism and literature, the residence at Southampton and the courtship of his future wife, of military service and marriage, of the long association with Pommery champagne, and later the foundation and development of the Wine and Food Society.

The last chapter, entitled 'Farewell', is so expressive of André's philosophy, his religious faith and his happy outlook on life that it demands extensive treatment.

'And now, patient reader,' the chapter begins, 'I will attempt to sum up my life's philosophy before we part company.

'I believe that God Almighty has given us life that we may be happy, praise Him and thank Him with a joyful heart, and not to have our fill of misery and curse the day when we were born.

'It must surely be possible to go to Heaven without having made our life on earth as near Hell as we could. I know that Our Lord died upon the Cross for us and that Christians should walk in the footsteps of Christ, but His footsteps led to Cana in Galilee before the last journey to Calvary. God in His mercy has given me a seat at the marriage feast, no water but my fill of good wine, and when my Cross comes before I die I mean to accept it as gratefully as the many joys of my long life.'

Joy, continues André, is not a sin but a blessing. It is a holy command. 'Look through Holy Writ and you will find many more *Hosannas* and *Alleluias*, *Gaudete* and *Laetare* than penitential lamentations.' Why, he asks, has he been blessed with so much more joy for so many more years than so many better men? 'I cannot tell. I do not know. But I refuse to believe that because I have hardly had a pain or an ache in eighty years I must be prepared to pay for it after death.'

From this point he expounds his views on *joie de vivre*, and in doing so turns on the puritanical outlook that was to him the prime enemy of good living. 'There are, I know, good people, highly moral and well-meaning people for whom the very name *la joie de vivre* is immoral. They look upon the slightest gratification of the senses as sinful: they merely "eat to live" and they are sorry for poor brutes like myself who know no better and who live to eat. I have no patience with them because I look upon them as heretics who do not accept the orthodox ruling that God's gifts are all good gifts which we have no more right to ignore than to abuse or misuse. To shut one's eyes to beauty or one's nostrils to truffles is sheer puritanical heresy.'

Not all rejection of the Good Life, however, is puritanical or heretical; and a notable passage follows in which André undoubtedly had in mind his own children and the path they had chosen in life:

> But there are others who have no interest whatever in any *joie de vivre*. They are the chosen few who have renounced the world the better to serve God: they are the small élite to whom has been given a foretaste on earth of the divine love that passes all understanding. It is not sympathy that I have for them but the most sincere admiration. They are the salt of the earth and there is very little salt to a great deal of earth.

Most of us, however, have to live in the world, and André argues robustly that there is no reason whatever why we should make ourselves unhappy about it. But we must use the gifts we have received to the maximum of our ability. 'Rich or poor, young or old, it is our bounden duty to make the best possible use of the life that has been given to us on loan. But how can we do so unless we are taught to know, to use and to perfect the tools which have been given us by a merciful Providence, chief among them our various senses and the master-key of the brain? . . . Most of us have been given normal senses and it is up to us to train them, to make them all the more sensitive, hence more helpful. But do we? It is only too true that, in the spiritual sense, many have eyes who will not see and have ears who will not hear: but there are many more who have a nose and will not smell and who have a palate but will not taste, in the physical sense.'

This brings him back to the religious aspect of life. For to André there is an even greater sin than misuse of the senses, the besetting sin of the age, ingratitude to God for the gifts and graces received. 'God asks but little of us: just to say "Please" whenever we want anything within reason – for what else is a prayer but an earnest "Please, Sir!"? And we are also expected to say "Thank you" for favours received. But who bothers to do so? Far too few.'

And so to the peroration of this noble exposition of man's duty to his maker:

I believe in peace on earth to all men of goodwill, but only if and when we remember the first command of the Christmas message, 'Glory be to God in the Highest'.

Life is a gift which we share with the grass and the beasts of the fields: they return no thanks and sing no praises; they know no better, but I do and I thank God the Giver every day for His many gifts, for the blessing of the beloved partner who has shared my long life, for our five children, and our many good friends, and also for much good wine and good food gratefully received and thoroughly enjoyed.

André, it is clear, thought of *By Request* as his *Nunc dimittis*. But a decade and more were still to pass before the time would come for the final departure.

Nonagenarian

As the 1950s merged into the 1960s, and André progressed through his eighties, some slowing up was inevitable. But in his case it was not very obtrusive. His palate
was as acute as ever, and he still revelled in good food and
good wine. His vitality was proof against the mere advance of
old age. And his happy outlook on life was invincible. He
remained the best of company.

The Wine and Food Society, of which he remained in
control, had taken on a new lease of life. Membership
increased, and in this period it was as prosperous as it had
ever been, bringing in a comfortable income for its president.
Critics were not lacking who thought this income too comfortable; the Society and its profits, some considered, had
remained too much of a one-man concern. But to André the
position was simple. The Wine and Food Society was his
creation and his property, and he was fully entitled to treat it
as such. He was, as one of his old friends testifies, a 'tough
nut' when it came to money.

Certainly he did his full share of the work. Marjorie
Fletcher looked after the administrative routine, but it was
André who devised the quarterly programme and took the
leading part in arranging the functions. And there was a
constant round of lunches, dinners and tastings to testify to
his hard work and his ingenuity.

He and Edith spent most of the week in London, and
guests were as frequent as ever at Evelyn Mansions. For

weekends there was Little Hedgecourt. Jeanne, a widow now, was in permanent residence there, and her brother André joined her when he was not busy in London; he was well established as an independent wine merchant. To Jeanne and André their parents were the most welcome of guests.

To André his eldest daughter had always been his favourite, and at this time he was probably closer to her than he had ever been since her marriage. She was an excellent hostess, and at his old house which was now for all purposes hers he was still able to entertain his friends with the best of good fare and good bottles.

With his elder son relations were a little more equivocal. André the younger, who grew to look more and more like his father as time went on, was a more volatile character than other members of the family. His private life was chequered, and his first two marriages both broke up. This was naturally a matter of pain to his parents, devout Catholics that they were and devoted to the ideal of the family unit. One friend who had known young André when they were both boys recalled that at a dinner, when he had not seen any of the family for some time, he was placed next to Madame Simon. Innocently to open the conversation he asked after her son. The response was that she immediately burst into a flood of tears and said: 'Oh dear, he has got divorced again.'

There were also slight complications in the business sphere. André *fils* called his wine firm by his own name, but on the label of his bottles appeared the signature 'André L. Simon'; and to those who knew the family the handwriting was unmistakably that of André *père*. This raised eyebrows, and led to contrasting accusations. On the one hand it was said that André was profiting from his son's business, with which in fact he had no connection; on the other that the younger André was battening on his father's reputation. There was perhaps a modicum of truth in both allegations;

- 174 -

but it does not appear that any ill-gotten gains accrued to the elder André. There are reasons for believing that the use of the signature was more of an embarrassment to him than anything else.

André was as tolerant a man as could be found, and as affectionate a father. He never allowed matters such as these to cause any rift with his son. He was always on good terms with his daughters-in-law, and it was a comfort to him that when André *fils* acquired his third wife, Janette or Jan, the marriage was and remained an ideally happy one. Jan became a close companion of his old age, and this time he was able to rejoice in the company of grandchildren.

To André, as to most men of his age, there came the grief of parting from old companions. Many of the cronies of his younger days had passed on, and they continued to do so; but some still lived, and André was not the man to relinquish a friendship once formed. Horace Annesley Vachell had died in 1955 at the ripe age of ninety-four. Almost to the end he had continued to correspond with his old companion, and André from time to time managed to visit him at Widcombe Manor.

Warner Allen was still alive, and as late as the beginning of 1963, in a letter from his home at Wallingford, he alluded to both of their careers and their reputations. 'You are indeed the Grand Old Man of Wine' was his tribute. 'If you are four years older in age than I am, you are many years younger in spirit and I excuse myself by the thought that, living in the wine world, you have been able to absorb more of the spirit of the grape in its finest form than I have, a mere tourist in that enchanted land, fortunate though I have been in my excursions.'

Ian Campbell, who for so long had formed, with Francis Berry and André, a triumvirate of the wine world, was also still alive, though in frail health and in complete retirement. Campbell had a gallant soldier son, whose services in the

1939–45 war had been honoured with the highest of all awards for bravery. Brigadier Lorne Campbell, VC, of the Argyll and Sutherland Highlanders, became a valued correspondent of André Simon in his old age. On 19 February 1954 he wrote:

> Lockhill
> Stubbs Wood
> Chesham Bois, Bucks

Dear Monsieur Simon,

Father has asked me to write to you as I am very sorry to say that he has had a slight heart attack and will have to take things easy for a bit. I am afraid the doctor won't allow him up to London at present, so he hopes you will not mind if he asks for his meeting with you to be temporarily postponed. He is very sorry about this as he was looking forward to it.

He is getting on all right, but will have to go slow and probably lie up for a little time. But he still remains very cheerful and makes light of it all.

I hope you are keeping well yourself.

> Yours very sincerely,
> Lorne

André's deep religious faith had if anything deepened with the years. Sister Marcelle of Jesus writes of his 'Christlike attitude in every circumstance'. 'I never', she adds, 'heard him say an uncharitable word about anyone or anything.'

Charity was indeed an essential part of his life. He had never relinquished his interest in the French Benevolent Society. Thursday was the day devoted to the *Bienfaisance*, as the charity and its activities were known in the Simon family. On this day he never went to any social function or had guests at Evelyn Mansions. Instead, on finishing work at his own office, he went to the society's headquarters at

41 Fitzroy Square to meet members of the French poor in London; he would listen to their tales of woe and allocate funds for cases which had come up during the week and were referred to him by the staff. He would get home about 7.30 p.m., and his daughter Madeleine recalls that these were the only occasions on which she saw him looking really weary.

At Christmas a number of shops donated food to the society, and a display was held in Fitzroy Square to which the needy were invited to come. Each was given a bottle of wine and a small or large bag (according to whether it was for a family, a couple or an individual) which they filled as they chose from the dainties on display. Madeleine remembers driving her father on Christmas Eve in a car packed with parcels for those too old or too ill to collect for themselves.

These French exiles were simple souls, quite unequal to looking after their own interests. André used to tell the family of '*une pauvre vieille*' who was given a weekly donation of 10s., week in, week out, and still seemed in utter poverty. One Thursday one of the Benevolent Society's staff at 41 Fitzroy Square followed her out, and saw her post her gift in the nearest pillar box. She apparently thought she was getting post office savings.

Much of the money thus doled out, it is clear, came from André's own pocket; but his own family always came first. Sister Marcelle recalls that her father could never keep any money in his pocket. Many applicants arrived at his office and were never sent away empty-handed. 'His friends used to tell him that many were rogues; if he found that they were he did not repeat his alms, but he said that he could never refuse a first appeal.'

'At one time,' adds Marcelle, 'when the financial outlook was not good, he still continued his charities until Mother told him that he would have us on the streets; to which he replied, "You have never wanted for anything yet, have you?" And she had to admit that she never had.'

On the surface life seemed to be going smoothly enough for the valiant old gentleman. But there was a cloud, and a black one, on the horizon. For as the decade of the 1960s approached the health of Edith Simon began to fail.

She too was over eighty, and she had not the strength or the resilience of her sturdy husband. Her main trouble was a narrowing of the arteries to the legs, resulting in the cutting off of the blood supply. She was moved into the Middlesex Hospital, and there she had to have the worse affected of her legs amputated. The operation was successful, but she was miserable in hospital without André, and as soon as possible he got her home. She had to have day and night nurses: a considerable expense, but to André all that mattered was that he should have her with him and be able to give her every help in her hour of need.

Characteristically she rallied, and to the delight of all her friends she was able to attend the Wine and Food Society's dinner held to celebrate her and André's diamond wedding on 17 October 1960. It was held at the Dorchester Hotel, and those who were present will remember the applause that greeted her when, in response to the health drunk to her and her husband, she was able to stand up in her place and bow to the company.

There followed two years and more of declining health and increased suffering. Under the influence of pain Edith developed an irascibility that seemed foreign to her temperament. An old friend recalls being embarrassingly present when, in a sudden tirade against André, she accused him of having a mistress. Never before had it been suggested that he had ever had any extra-marital love affair, and it was hardly likely that he would have embarked on one in his eighties.

Nevertheless this raises the question whether, in their long life together, he was ever unfaithful to his much loved wife. There is no evidence that he was. He loved feminine company, and basked in feminine admiration. But that, it would appear, is as far as it went.

Against this it must be recorded that a prominent lady journalist claimed that once, when being driven with him from East Grinstead to London, she had 'pretty well to fight for her innocence' most of the way. This again was in his old age, and the narrator of the story agrees that the lady in question was prone to exaggeration. Probably a few playful gallantries were all that were involved.

Edith's health continued to ebb away, and the time came when she had to be moved once again to the Middlesex Hospital, there to await the end. It came peacefully on 22 April 1963.

She had her family around her. Her Carmelite daughter Marcelle, allowed by her convent in Yorkshire to go to her mother's bedside, recalls the final moments. 'Her last words on earth were nothing pious; she just looked at my father standing by her, said "Wonderful husband", and went peacefully to God.'

To André the blow was devastating. He had lost his sheet-anchor, the beloved companion who had shared his life for more than sixty years. 'We had loved one another,' he wrote in his final volume of memoirs, 'we had understood and helped one another the whole of our lives. Now the end had come.'

Yet even now he rallied. His resilience was proof against even the deepest private sorrow. 'I had to have a change,' we read in *In the Twilight*; 'a real change. I was only eighty-six, without a pain or an ache, quite as fit as men I knew who were twenty years younger. I had sold my Quarterly Magazine *Wine and Food* to Condé Nast, and I reckoned that I could afford to go round the world, mostly by sea to Australia and San Francisco, by air to New York, and by a Cunarder back to Southampton.'

The sale of *Wine and Food* is another action of André's that has aroused great criticism. The magazine, it is claimed with reason, was the property of the Wine and Food Society; yet André disposed of it for his own private profit. Yet to André once again the issue was simple. He owned the Society, and he owned its magazine. He was entitled to do what he liked with them. At any rate the sale provided him with money with which to carry out his travel programme. And this programme nobody could begrudge him.

The programme was duly carried out, though not exactly as first planned. Among the numerous notes and jottings left by André at Little Hedgecourt is a long handwritten record of his final travels, clearly intended to have formed a chapter in the further volume of autobiography which he now had in mind. It is headed, characteristically, 'Three Journeys before the Last'.

Towards the end of 1963 he sailed in the *Canberra* for Australia. It was a good voyage, and he was greatly impressed with the liner and its catering arrangements:

The Canberra was a marvellous ship, a floating city with some 2000 men, women and children of various races and creeds to be fed daily according to their particular religion, tradition, or mere fancy, and what about water for such a crowd to wash and to drink? No problem! No shortage of water in the sea and the Canberra daily pumped aboard tons of water from the sea, got the salt and all else out of it, so that there was enough water and to spare for washing and cooking. But they did something more wonderful still! They added something to the desalted sea water and made it quite good drinking. I certainly would never have believed possible that the day would come, and it did, when I would drink sea water and enjoy it! I had a most comfortable cabin, and a very good cabin steward, Mass every morning in the Cinema, very fair meals and wines.

Some pleasant fellow-passengers, and, on the whole, quite an enjoyable voyage.

It was André's first visit to Australia. He reached Perth on 10 December, and it was there that he changed his plans. An outline of his travel arrangements had been printed in *Wine and Food*, and the result was that letters now reached him from some of the American Wine and Food Society chapters asking him to visit them before going to New York and home. 'This meant hopping about the North American Continent from the Canadian border to New Orleans, which I could not afford to do, or else calling at two or three places on the way to New York, such as Kansas City and Chicago, which meant hurting the feelings of a number of others.'

Consequently he decided to cancel his Cunard booking from New York to Southampton and return to England in the *Canberra*. He had a circular letter sent to all the American chapters informing them that he would pay a last visit to the United States in 1966; he would go to whatever city they chose, stay there, and be glad to welcome anybody who would like to meet him then. The Americans warmly agreed to the plan, and in due course the choice for the rendezvous was made; the city would be Chicago.

Meanwhile André was enjoying the Australian scene and making new friends. At Perth he was met by a 'a pleasant, youngish man' who introduced himself as Henry Stone and told him he had been a devoted disciple of his for years. Stone drove him to his home in Perth, and then to a winery a few miles away where he had a whole range of Australian wines for the master to taste.

Re-embarking in the *Canberra*, André was soon on the way to Melbourne, arriving there at noon on 13 December. He was met by Victor Gibson, president of the Melbourne Wine and Food Society, whom he had met once before in London, and who drove him straight to Antonio's Restaurant.

Antonio's opened in the evening only and served dinners and suppers but no lunch. 'But on December 13th 1963 Antonio served a de luxe luncheon for members of the Wine and Food Societies of Victoria and no one else. We sat down 58, men only, about half of them members of the Melbourne Society and the rest from Societies from 30 to 300 miles from Melbourne, but all in Victoria.'

Next came Sydney, where the *Canberra* berthed at midnight on 16 December. When André landed the next morning, there was Sir James McGregor, a friend of long standing, to welcome him. Jim McGregor took him around Sydney and the neighbourhood, and there followed another round of lunches, dinners and tastings.

A surprise that gave him peculiar pleasure came when he was guest of honour at a Sydney Wine and Food Society tasting. 'One of the members introduced himself to me and told me that his name was Arthur Sutton. It did not ring a bell. Then he handed to me a small paperback booklet, and I could hardly believe my eyes when I read "Somewhere in Flanders, by A.L.S., May 1916". In May 1916 Sutton was serving with an Australian unit in Flanders next to the 50th Division (Northumbrian) to which I was attached as interpreter. I had the little book privately printed for my friends in the 50th Division as a souvenir of our various places of fighting and of rest in Flanders before we moved down to Armentières and Arras. I certainly never dreamed that I would see a copy nearly 50 years later, and in Sydney!'

André was in Sydney when the new year came, and on the last day of 1963 he had a fresh experience when he sat down to lunch as the only male with eleven ladies. Neville Baker, whom he describes as one of the finest amateur cooks he had ever known, had a few days before entertained him to a meal for men only at his home on Cherry Hill, St Ives; on this occasion the guests were waited on by Mrs Baker and the wives of some of the guests. André made some remark about this being unfair to the ladies, whereupon Baker invited him to come again on 31 December. When he arrived, Baker greeted him with the words: 'You will be happy today. We shall wait upon the ladies for a change.' And so it was; André, with Mrs Baker on his right, was the only man at table, and he and the ladies were served by Neville Baker and his friends.

That night the company saw the new year in with Krug 1955 champagne.

There followed visits to Brisbane and to Canberra, where Sir Robert Menzies was a fellow-guest at a dinner of the local Wine and Food Society; Sir Robert was to become, and remain, a devoted friend. Then back to Melbourne for more tours of Victorian vineyards and wineries. This time André's principal guides and hosts were his good friend Victor Gibson, president of the Melbourne Wine and Food Society, and his wife Madge. In Melbourne he attended 'the largest and best banquet of the Wine and Food Societies in Australia', with Victor Gibson in the chair and the Governor of Victoria as chief guest. 'I remember walking back to the Melbourne Club at a very late hour, quite fit and more surprised than proud at it.'

Ballarat came next, and then, with Victor and Madge Gibson, André flew to Adelaide, which he made his headquarters for visiting the vineyards and wineries of South Australia. From there the Gibsons flew back to Melbourne, and André to Sydney.

This crowded tour culminated in a visit to New Zealand, where André flew from Sydney. There he was entertained as lavishly as he had been anywhere in Australia, thanks mainly to Frank Thorpy, a real enthusiast, who had been the pioneer of gastronomy in the islands and who still, twenty years after André's visit, is the presiding genius there of wine and food. Of his attentions André could not speak too warmly. 'At Auckland Frank did not give me the guest room in his small house by the sea. He gave me his own room and moved into the guest room, which was not just kindness but devotion.'

Both at Auckland and at Wellington André met old friends and made new ones. At the latter centre he renewed acquaintance with Harry Moss, who had been a colleague as an agent of Pommery in days of long ago. 'But it was Frank Thorpy, who had welcomed me on the tarmac of the Auckland airport, who saw me off back to Sydney on the tarmac of the Wellington airport.'

Returning to Sydney, he found a letter awaiting him from Kevin Healy, president of Western Australia's Wine and Food Society, informing him that the *Canberra* (with André on board) was due to berth at Fremantle on 28 February 1964, which he knew would be the traveller's eighty-seventh birthday. The Western Australian Society invited him to be their guest at a lunch in Perth on that day, and to bring with him any friends he might have in or near the town. He replied that one of his best friends would be in the neighbourhood on that day; this was the captain of the *Canberra*, Harry Stone, and he would be happy to have him at the lunch. So long as he saw Stone there, he would know that the *Canberra* would not sail without him.

Thus it was arranged. The birthday lunch was a great success, André sitting between the president of the Society and the captain of the ship that had brought him from Sydney. Afterwards Stone saw him on board the *Canberra* and that evening entertained him with fish that had been caught and vegetables that had been picked that day.

So ended the great tour, certainly one of the most memorable that André ever made in his long life. It must have been a considerable strain on his constitution, but he showed little sign of this when he arrived back in London in March. And there was no doubt that it helped to soothe his aching heart. André is recorded as saying that if it were not for his faith he could never have accepted the loss of his wife. His religious faith had unquestionably the deepest influence on him, but one may accept that the heart-warming experiences of his busy and extensive tour of far-away Australia also played their part in helping him to acquiesce in his lot.

There were still two more major voyages to follow 'before the last'. But in the meantime there was a shorter trip – to André's native country in the summer of 1964. It was memorable mainly for the circumstance that it marked the final reconciliation with the champagne firm of Pommery et Greno.

The initiator was André's great friend George Rainbird, author and publisher, who was now taking an increasingly important part in the affairs of the Wine and Food Society. He was working on his authoritative book on the history of champagne, and he persuaded his friend and mentor to accompany him to France for some up-to-the-minute research.

The head of Pommery was now the Prince Guy de Polignac, cousin of the Marquis Melchior who thirty years earlier had deprived André of his agency. André and his friend arranged with the Prince for a visit to the firm's cellars in Rheims.

Let George Rainbird himself tell the story:

It was a very nostalgic experience, that six-day tour, for André, and I remember quite a few incidents arising out of it. I learned a lot about André, and champagne. The food, of course, was of the very first order, and the champagne was the best that the great champagne houses could pro-duce, which is saying quite a lot. And as André said one evening, 'the champagne corks have been popping like machine guns for some days now. It's time I had a rest.'

André always retained his love of Pommery, as he well might. And the Pommerys could not do enough for André.

I remember that André wanted to go down into the cellars as he had done twice a day in his apprenticeship and also climbed up something like 184 steps in the evenings. And the Prince de Polignac gave him a sumptuous villa luncheon, with the best champagne that Pommery's could produce. And then we went off to catch the train to Paris because Pommery had been left to the end of the tour. The Prince de Polignac insisted on carrying André's baggage from the car to the train, stowing it away, and seeing that André was quite comfortable. And so ended that chapter.

It was in April of this year, 1964, that André was made an honorary Commander of the Order of the British Empire. This CBE had to be 'honorary' because, through all his years of residence in England, he had never renounced his French citizenship. But the distinction gave him great pleasure. In the days of World War I he had been awarded the Military Medal by George V. Now, nearly half a century later, he was honoured with a further decoration by King George's granddaughter. He had been for many years an *Officier* of the *Légion d'Honneur* of France.

Just a year after embarking on his gruelling but rewarding tour of Australia and New Zealand, André set out on the second of the Three Journeys. This time it was to South Africa.

It was a less ambitious venture than the first. André had been to the country many times before; there were no new places to explore. But the pattern was of a similar nature. Everywhere he went he met old friends and made new ones. And the branches of the Wine and Food Society that had sprung up in the post-war years vied with each other in doing honour to their venerable founder.

He had intended to travel alone; but by chance Albert Guillet, his daughter Jeanne's brother-in-law, was going on the same route to visit his son, daughter-in-law and grandson

in Durban, and the two travelled together from Southampton to Cape Town. Albert had been heavily involved in
the sad events of 1932–3, but all grievances were set aside
now. And so once more there was a satisfying reconciliation.

At Cape Town André was the guest of the KWV, the
initials by which the Cape Wine Growers' Co-operative
Association was known; and there he was welcomed on the
Association's behalf by Mrs Mulder, who took a leading part
in business affairs in the district. A singularly happy
friendship was immediately formed. For the rest of the tour
Zita Mulder made it her particular mission to look after her
distinguished guest, watching over his welfare with such care
and devotion that he called her his 'Little Mother'. And as
such he knew her to the end of his life.

He stayed at the Mount Nelson Hotel, which he had
known for thirty years and more, and there he was greeted
with an official luncheon given by the Cape wine trade.
Thereafter he made his headquarters at Lanzerac, near
Stellenbosch, and from there he travelled to all the
main centres of the wine trade, always honoured and fêted
with the maximum of gastronomic splendour, and always
accompanied by his Little Mother, Zita Mulder.

So once again André had his birthday celebrations in a
distant clime. 'My eighty-eighth birthday', he wrote in *In the
Twilight*, 'was something that I had never heard of or expected, let alone deserved. It lasted three days. On Saturday,
27 February 1965, the Guild of Wine Tasters of the Cape
gave me a birthday eve banquet in the banqueting chamber
of the Cape Town City Hall; the next day, Sunday, the Cape
Town Wine and Food Society gave me a champagne birthday
luncheon at Lanzerac, where I was staying as the guest of
Sawfa (South Africa Wine Farmers' Association); and on the
next day, Monday, 1 March, Sawfa gave a remarkable
banquet at their Paarl headquarters. A gala performance
deserving full marks!'

Thus did South Africa bid its final farewell to the father-figure who had done so much to further its wine production and wine trade. A few weeks later he was back in London, still pursuing with zest and energy the activities of the Wine and Food Society.

One of his first acts on returning home was to send a copy of *By Request* to Zita Mulder. Her letter of thanks is worth quoting:

My dearest André,

You are kind, kind, kind – that is why so many people love you. You knew that I would love to have your autobiography so you sent me 'By Request'. This has brought me great happiness because, although you are a world figure, you became my friend and we enjoyed simple things together . . . This makes life.

Your inscription in the book 'to my little mother' is the greatest compliment you could ever have paid me. Remember, if you are 6, 60, or 88, you are still my little boy who has to be in bed by 10 p.m. Even if I am not there to see this, I would want you to listen to my advice – merely because you endeared yourself to me and because I am concerned about your well-being.

Please, when you see your children, tell them of me and my regard for you because I know that you have allowed each one to find their happiness and fulfilment in the way they saw best and you have not stood in their way. This is the stamp of greatness.

It was the greatest moment of my life meeting you and, although it might only have been an incident in your very full life, to me it is an experience which will live with me to the end of my days.

Bless you, my dear, and again many thanks for the book.

Much love,
Zita

I recall the last personal talk I ever had with André, which must have been about this time. It was a chance brief encounter, and it was connected with a temporary crisis in my own family.

My brother, Dermot Morrah, whom many will remember as for many years chairman of the Wine Society, had suffered a severe heart attack. He was at the time living close to Westminster Cathedral, and I in Dolphin Square. André of course was at Evelyn Mansions; so the three of us were close neighbours.

Dermot was taken to Westminster Hospital, where for a time his life was in grave danger. He rallied, but had a sudden relapse one evening, just as I arrived at the hospital to visit him. I managed to get in touch with my sister-in-law, who had gone home, and she came in haste to her husband's side. We both stayed there all night, expecting the worst all the time; but the patient weathered the storm, and as day dawned I decided to walk home to Dolphin Square.

As I approached Westminster Cathedral I saw tottering (for he tottered now) towards me from the other side a well-known figure. It was André making his way from Evelyn Mansions to the cathedral for his daily 7 a.m. Mass.

We stopped and talked, and I told him what the situation was. He listened with the deepest sympathy.

'How old is your brother?' he asked me.

I told him: 'Sixty-nine.'

'Ah, he is twenty years younger than I am,' was his comment. 'He will get over it.'

A thoughtful pause. Then: 'Would your sister-in-law like some wine?'

I said I was sure she would. Before the day was out a case of claret had arrived at my brother's flat.

André's judgement was correct. Dermot lived for another nine years.

The last of the three great journeys 'before the last' took place in 1966. It was a much shorter and quicker affair than the other two, but memorable none the less.

André had promised to go once more to America, and to meet members of the various Wine and Food Society chapters in Chicago. Plans for this event grew with the months and years, and the assembly developed into what became known as the first international convention of what was soon to be known as the International Wine and Food Society.

The other voyages had been by sea. This one was by air; in May he flew to Chicago. He had meant to go on his own, but those around him thought it wiser that, in his ninetieth year, he should have a close companion on the flight. His daughter-in-law Janette, the younger André's wife, was invited to accompany him, and she was only too glad to accept. André was delighted with her company.

There were others too. This meeting was recognised as an important official event in the affairs of the Society, and several members of the London committee, including George Rainbird, were in the party.

The convention marked the beginning of a great expansion of the Society in the United States; expansion which has gone on from that time to this. The American chapters were reorganised under a North American committee headed by Dr George H. Rezek, an indefatigable enthusiast who worked day and night for the convention's success. Rezek's efforts were rewarded. The convention was a triumph for all concerned, and a particular joy to the venerable founder of the Wine and Food Society; his American friends and disciples were overjoyed to have him among them, and entertained him with all the lavishness at their disposal.

'Thanks to the energy, vision and optimism of Dr George Rezek and a devoted team of hard-working helpers', wrote André, 'the Convention was a great success and it gave me much pleasure to see once more a few of my old American friends such as Roy Alciatore, all the way from New Orleans, Maynard Amerine from California, Paul Spitler and Harold Grossman, from New York, both of whom now are no more; as well as a number of younger friends from the USA and other parts of the world, including two delegates from Tokio. I was able to attend and enjoy luncheons, dinners and tastings like all delegates, talk as much as any of them, if not more.'

André's travels were over. He never left Europe again. But there was one more great celebration in store. On 28 February 1967 he would complete his ninetieth year.

In the meantime he founded a new dining club. It was a small and intimate affair; members dined in each other's houses, and there were never more than half a dozen at a time. But they included some of his closest friends in the wine world. One was Vyvyan Holland; another George Rainbird. There were also Dr Walter Somerville, Eustace Hoare and Raymond Bantock. The club was given the name of *Les Grands Crus*.

It lived up to its title. André saw to it that only the finest vintages graced the meals.

They were pleasant occasions. Dr Somerville recalls that André took the lead in discussing the wines served. He was always succinct, informative, and to the point; never repetitive.

And so the great day approached. Friends all over the world prepared to do honour to their venerable mentor, the supreme patron of wine and gastronomy. The Wine and Food Society of course took the lead, and it was decided to hold the birthday banquet at the Dorchester.

The menu for this truly memorable meal ran as follows:

Chicken broth

Scotch Salmon with Champagne sauce

Roast saddle of lamb, peas and new potatoes

Wensleydale cheese

Apple pie and cream

Coffee

A simple enough English dinner. But every dish was of the highest quality.

Naturally enough it was the wines that made the meal most memorable. Gifts of wine had poured in on André from all parts of the world, and some of them were served on this occasion. It was appropriate that a present of a particularly distinctive Pommery champagne had come from Prince Guy de Polignac. The list at the dinner was:

Champagne: Avize 1961 (Pommery & Greno)

La Riva Amontillado Extra 1819

Pouilly-Fuissé Château Fuissé Le Clos 1959

Château Pichon-Longueville Baron 1953

Château Latour 1929

Champagnes aux Grandes Marques
Vintages 1959 or 1961

Cognac Camus: 'Hors d'Ages'

The authoritative summing-up of this splendid evening comes from the pen of Julian Jeffs QC, close friend of André and himself the author of the classic English work on sherry. He wrote in *Wine and Food*:

André Simon's 90th birthday party was a memorable banquet. It seems astonishing that any hotel, however good, could serve a meal of really high quality to over five hundred guests. But the Dorchester could and did. It seems even more astonishing that great wines should have been available for the same number, but again they were, thanks to the endeavours of the Wine and Food Society and the goodwill of André's many friends in the trade. The Chef de Cuisine was E. Kaufeler. Apart from many old friends, several members of the Simon family were present, including Father Peter Simon, S.J., one of his sons, who said grace.

The menu was a tribute to British gastronomy. It was also an inspired menu in that it consisted of food which could be prepared in such large quantities without sacrificing quality and which, in its simplicity, was calculated to show the fine wines to the very best advantage . . .

The Pommery & Greno, Avize, 1961, was a great rarity: a champagne from a single vineyard. And it was as exquisite as it was rare. For my own taste it was perhaps a trifle young, but few, I think, share my passion for old champagne. The sherry was superb: all that an old amontillado could possibly be. The pouilly-fuissé perfectly partnered the salmon and served as an admirable break between the assertive excellence of the sherry and the two fine clarets. Of these, the Château Pichon-Longueville Baron was a beautiful example of a classic claret of the 1953 vintage, still full of youth and admirably balanced. Opinions differed slightly as to the 1929 Château Latour, and one would expect a considerable difference between individual bottles of such an aged wine. There may have been one or two bottles which disappointed, but that served at the table on which I was sitting was impeccable: a perfect claret on top of its form. The 1959 champagnes were perfect, cheering wines to drink the toasts in.

André's health was proposed by the French Ambassador, Monsieur de Courcel, and André replied with all his old grace, eloquence and humour. A telegram from the Queen was read by George Rainbird, who said also that telegrams had been received from Wine and Food Society branches all over the world.

At the end of the evening André was a tired man. But he stayed to a late hour, signing menus at the emptying tables for his friends.

The great banquet at the Dorchester was followed by countless others all over the western world, as all the branches of the Society carried out their plans to honour their founder. Page after page in *Wine and Food* is devoted to details of these dinners and lunches. In Australia, which he had visited for the first time so recently, there were celebration meals in Sydney, Melbourne, Adelaide, Perth, Ballarat, Geelong and Brisbane; in Canada at Calgary and Vancouver; in New Zealand at Auckland and Christchurch. Nairobi, Hong Kong, Singapore, Kuala Lumpur, Tokyo and Salisbury (Rhodesia) supplied their gastronomic quota. In the United States the list was formidable, including all the chapters in whose foundation he had so delighted and which looked to him as their father and their friend.

At home in Britain it was the same story. If any branch failed to join in the celebrations, its identity cannot be traced.

Some of these functions were attended by André himself. Hugo Dunn-Meynell, now the leading figure in the International Wine and Food Society, recalls:

One he did go to was organised by the Surrey Branch. I was deputed to fetch him. I called at Evelyn Mansions at 11 as instructed, to find the old man asleep in a chair. His housekeeper absolutely forbade me to wake him, and as the clock progressed to 12, I got more and more worried. At 12.15 he woke up, upbraided us both for not calling him, and with surprising agility got into my brand-new Citroën Déesse of which I was rather proud. On the journey to Cobham it developed a fault of some kind, but I just drove on, terrified of André missing the party if I so much as stopped to see what the trouble was. He was very talkative, and my (secret) concentration on the mechanical problems must have made me seem bad company!

The lunch was a great success.

Afterwards André demanded to come home with me to tea; my wife didn't like me arriving with casual visitors, so – on the pretext of petrol – I stopped to telephone. She wasn't keen on the idea, but it didn't matter as when I returned to the car André was fast alseep, and he didn't wake up till we got back to his flat.

There were of course celebrations within the Simon circle as well. This time let Sister Madeleine tell the story. 'At a family party to celebrate his 90th birthday,' she writes, 'André Simon Fils produced a very old wine for the occasion, so old that it might have been excellent or it might have been quite undrinkable. It turned out to be excellent. I noticed that Pa had dropped out of the conversation and was caressing his glass. I asked him for his thoughts and he said that he was thinking with wonder that the acid from the earth and the sugar from the sun had been fighting for ascendancy in the bottle for all these years, but the balance of rain and sunshine that year must have been so perfect that neither had won, to turn the wine either into vinegar or into sugar. This was a real aesthetic joy to him.'

The whole collective programme added up to a grand culmination of André Simon's gastronomic career. Ninety years of age and a universally venerated figure, he decided it was time for him to say goodbye to the London scene.

Twilight and After

IN March 1967, just a month after André's ninetieth birthday, the lease of No. 6 Evelyn Mansions came to an end. He was not interested in renewal; for the years remaining to him his only address would be Little Hedgecourt in Sussex.

Before he finally left London there was at least one more memorable meal in honour of his birthday. The dinner at the Dorchester had been the Wine and Food Society's main tribute to its founder and president, but a few of his intimate friends in the Society wanted to pay their respects at a smaller, more personal function. This was arranged by senior members of the committee, with George Rainbird at their head. It was decided that the dinner should take place on 8 March at the Connaught Hotel, always known for the excellence of its cuisine and a favourite haunt of André's.

Some twenty-four people attended, sitting at one long table. Most were senior gastronomes, but among the younger guests were Michael Broadbent and Hugh Johnson. Mr Broadbent has vivid memories of the function.

'Apart from the whole occasion,' he writes, 'what struck me most was that, even at the age of 90, after a lifetime of food and wine, André was still as enthusiastic as ever, and his lively and inquiring mind was much in evidence. I recall that a magnum of 1877 Lafite had been sent over from the Château for the occasion. There was also a magnum of 1877 Château Haut-Bailly, a relatively little-known red Graves. I was most struck, and have never forgotten: André, in his speech, made reference to this Haut-Bailly which, though not very well-known now, was in 1877 a considerably larger vineyard producing outstanding wine and in fact had won a gold medal for the best-kept vineyard in the whole of the Gironde department. He also said other things about the wine which I cannot recall, but I remember being struck that, at his age, he still had that vital spark of academic inquisitiveness which drove him to do research on the 1877 Graves and impart his knowledge to guests at the dinner party.'

After more than thirty years as presiding genius of the Wine and Food Society, André had now relinquished all share in its management. His successor as chairman was George Rainbird, who later recalled the process of transference of authority, in circumstances not in all ways satisfactory to himself:

The time came, round about the early sixties I suppose, when the National Magazine Company sold their offices, which André had had for some years, and he was by then over eighty. He became homeless and bemused at the thought of going round trying to find new offices for the Society. It just happened that I had moved my business into a very big house in Hyde Park Place and the first-floor drawing room was empty, with a small room for a secretary and so on, and I was able to offer this to André at the same rent that he had been paying the National Magazine Company, which I believe was then £600 a year. I gave him a lease which ran to the end of my own lease at the same price. This didn't work out, but we moved shortly afterwards to bigger premises in the Edgware Road, where I again accommodated him with the best offices in the place. The Society never paid more than £600 a year, and when that lease ended, and we moved again, it cost my firm

£15,000 to compensate the Society. On the whole, that was rather funny – but not at the time. Still, it makes me laugh.

It followed that with close proximity to one another in Hyde Park Place and later the Edgware Road, and with my natural interest in wine, I began to see more and more of André. He very shortly appointed me to the consulting council, as he called it, which was a misnomer. They were never consulted; André ran the whole show as he always had since the death of A. J. A. Symons.

Eventually I succeeded him as chairman of the Society, where I remained in office for about seven years.

Everything we had got was charged to the Society, and the great gastronomic library – probably the best in the world – belonged to the Society, and was acknowledged in print as such. But that did not stop him from selling it for his own private profit. The same thing happened with the Wine and Food Society's journal, which he sold, without telling me anything about it, to Condé Nast for, I think, £7,000, which he immediately invested in an annuity which went on for some years, long after the capital sum had been exhausted.

I don't grudge him any of this, but I must say that, when I took over the Society and discovered that he had withdrawn every penny of the Society's deposits from the Society's deposit and current accounts, and left me, as his successor, the princely sum of £1,000 to carry on the whole work of the Society, I was, like Queen Victoria, not amused.

But his integrity was absolute. He owned the Society, and therefore he owned everything in it, although he had publicly stated that the library belonged to the Society. However, he was a great man and I've never counted it against him. But that £1,000 stuck in my craw for a long time. In point of fact, and as the Society records can show,

I think the membership was between 2,000 and 3,000 when André left. When I left, seven years later, it had gone up to 6,000 or 7,000, or maybe more. Like André I travelled, but at my expense and not at the Society's. I never charged the Society with a penny.

The 'French peasant' element in André's character, on which so many of his old acquaintances have commented, was clearly much in evidence in this episode. It was part of the man, and those who had financial dealings with him had to accept it or break with him altogether, which few wanted to do. In the circumstances Mr Rainbird's forbearing comments must be accounted more than generous. But he was not alone in taking such an attitude.

And so came the final retirement to the Sussex countryside. At Little Hedgecourt, during those last few years, André Simon was tended with loving care by his beloved daughter Jeanne and by his daughter-in-law Jan, the wife of André *fils*. The younger André himself, a prosperous wine merchant in his late fifties now, was intermittently at the house.

André *père* was by no means inactive. The elder statesman *par excellence* of the gastronomic world, he was consulted by all and sundry on matters of wine and food. There were constant visits from friends old and new, and there were tastings and periodical meals of accustomed high quality. First-rate cuisine was to be found at Gravetye Manor, a country house in the neighbourhood converted into a restaurant, and there André repaired from time to time with his children and his friends.

New acquaintances were Victor Webb and his wife Joan who, resident in Bonn, there founded a Rhineland branch of the Wine and Food Society. It was the first of the Society's branches to be established on the European continent outside the United Kingdom.

At first the friendship existed by means of correspondence. Mr Webb preserves a handwritten letter, a model of neatness and legibility, which shows that André, shortly before his ninety-first birthday, had already made detailed plans for his hundredth:

> Little Hedgecourt
> East Grinstead
> Sussex
> 10/2/68

Dear Mr Webb

Many thanks for your letter of the 5th, the menu and newspaper cuttings referring to the inaugural Dinner of the Rhineland Branch. My hearty Congratulations upon the success of this function which does you and Mrs Webb great credit! In a world full of hatred, suffering and violence, how welcome it is to hear of such truly civilized and all too rare occasions when friends meet and relax, enjoying good fare and good wines and each other's company!

Many thanks also for your good wishes for my birthday. I do hope that you and Mrs Webb will be able to be in London for my Centenary! You will have some Château Margaux 1961 leading up to Château Latour 1945, as well as the top brands of 1961 Champagne, now 'surpointe', which will be disgorged in February 1977 for the Dinner! I'll do my best to be there myself!

> Yours sincerely
> André L. Simon

Up to this time his health had remained remarkably good, but in 1968 his sight began to fail. Once the rot had set in the trouble increased rapidly, and though opinions differ slightly it would appear that by the time his ninety-second birthday came round he was totally blind. Yet he was not daunted. It would take more than blindness to keep André Simon from his literary activity. For a time he went on writing in longhand, though often the words ran off the edge of the paper. When this became impossible he taught himself to use a typewriter, making himself before the end a reasonably skilful touch-typist. And it was at this time, when one would have expected him at last to sit back in comfortable relaxation, that he embarked on yet another book – his long-planned second volume of reminiscences.

Even with his new-found skills this would have been a formidable task indeed, which he could hardly have undertaken unaided. Fortunately he had the highly competent and devoted assistance of one of his youngest but most loyal friends and disciples.

Hugh Johnson, now well-known as a particularly eminent writer on wine, was in the late 1960s making his name in his chosen line. He was also a leading light in the management of the Wine and Food Society. André at this time became more than ever intimate with Hugh and with his wife and small daughter, and this intimacy continued until the end of his life.

The friendship is illustrated in a series of letters which are among the last from André's pen that can be traced. On 8 February 1967 he wrote inviting his young friend to the planned dinner at the Connaught:

My dear Hugh
    I want to give a chance to the members of the Dinner Committee to taste under the most suitable conditions some of the 1877 Clarets sent to me for my 90th Birthday. Of course, I hope that you will be able to be there? It will be at the Connaught Hotel on March 8th 7.30 for 8 p.m. Dinner jacket.

My love to you both
André

This letter, sent from Evelyn Mansions, is handwritten and shows no sign of eye trouble. The same may be said of a rather longer communication sent from East Grinstead just over a year later, on 15 February 1968, although in this he does allude to the disability that had now begun to overtake him:

My dear Hugh

So glad to hear that all is well with you, Judy and Lucy! Yes! I am sorry and somewhat ashamed to say that I caught another cold. But the first one, in 1915, was soon shaken off, whereas the second (present) one hangs on and on! So depressing!

28 Feb. – my birthday, happens to be Ash Wednesday, so the W. & F.S. Dinner will be on the 27th, Shrove Tuesday, at the Savoy. They have booked a suite at the Savoy for my daughter, who will see that my tie is tied properly, before we go down to dinner, and that I do not go to bed with my boots on after dinner – and for me!

We could drive direct from here to you on the 27th and back to the Savoy in the early afternoon for a rest before dinner. So simple and so tempting. But I am not too sure that it would be wise. I am getting old slowly but surely. My sight is failing and so is my strength. Which is what anybody would and must expect! . . .

My love to all three!

André

Others in the same vein follow, and it is not till 25 February 1969 that the first typewritten epistle appears, containing a few typing errors. Arrangements for the Johnson family to visit Little Hedgecourt were being made, and André wrote:

My dear High

Thank you for your good wishes! I am very sorry to hear of your father's death. He must have been much younger than I am (not as old as I am would be better!) He was so fit when we were fellow passengers on Canberra in 1964! Next Saturday would not be a good day as there is sickness in the house, but all should be well by Saturday 8th. I only hope that the sun will shine and that Lucy may pick her own wild daffodils. I have gone back to my old typewriter abd take my time as I cannot read what I write, so cannot possibly correct any od my mistakes. My love to Gudy and Lucy, please!

Yours
André

The correspondence went on almost till the end. The last letter in the series preserved by Mr Johnson is a short note dated 1 January 1970:

Dear Hugh, Judy and little Lucy

all my best wishes for your good health and much happiness during every one of the ten years of the Seventies – my last decade!

I am sorry to say that I have not been very well of late, but I am on the mend now!

With my love
André

The affectionate references to Lucy Johnson prompt the comment that all through his life André was fond of children, and when they came to know him they were equally fond of him. He knew how to win their confidence, and this aspect of his character grew stronger as he reached old age.

He loved his friends to bring their children to Little

Hedgecourt. Anthony Berry remembers thus taking his little daughter Gloria to call on his venerable friend.

André received her with the greatest pleasure. 'Now, my dear,' he said, 'come and sit by me and have a glass of champagne.'

So Gloria Berry, at the age of eight, enjoyed her first glass of champagne under the highest auspices.

Probably Lucy Johnson also indulged in champagne in the company of her distinguished friend. At any rate she and her parents were often at Little Hedgecourt, becoming almost members of the Simon family. And it was in these circumstances that Hugh Johnson gave to André the most invaluable help in the production of his final literary work. He was not exactly a collaborator. *In the Twilight* is the exclusive work of its author. But it could not have been achieved without Hugh Johnson, who acted as André's amanuensis, arranged the publication, read the proofs and saw the book through the press.

The publishers, through the good offices of George Rainbird, were Michael Joseph, and the book saw the light of day in 1969. The dedication read: *'Pour Jeanne ma fille aînée et bien-aimée'*; and the further inscription followed: 'I wish to record my grateful appreciation of the most valuable help given to me, in my near blindness, by my young and dear friend, Hugh Johnson, who has seen this book through the press.'

In the Twilight is not a work of straightforward autobiography as is *By Request*; not even an account of the years of his life passed since that book was written. Rather it is a series of essays dealing with various aspects of his career and filling in the gaps left in the earlier work. It tells of his foreign tours, of his appearances in the witness box when more than once he spoke up in court for the correct nomenclature of wines, of memorable meals, of the French Benevolent Society, and of the book collecting that was so dear to his heart. The whole volume amounts to a worthy memorial to a long life most satisfactorily and most enjoyably spent. The final valediction reads:

It was in 1968 that old age caught me at last.

No complaints! I am ready to go. I have had more than my fair share of all that is best – faith, affection, and good health, three wonderful gifts that no money can buy.

I have worked hard as long as I could see, and loved it. Even when I can no longer see, I cannot accept idleness. I am still writing in the twilight.

André was indeed ready to go. He was ninety-two years old, and for all his playful talk about celebrating his hundredth birthday he had not expected to live so long. The end could not be far off.

For a time the old routine still went on. His palate and his appetite seemed unimpaired, and he was still happy to go out for meals when any of his old friends turned up to take him. Michael Broadbent remembers one such occasion.

'A year or so after he gave up his London flat,' he writes, 'and lived at Little Hedgecourt, I heard that he was feeling lonely and rather out of things. By then he had relinquished hold on the Society.

'So I plucked up courage and arranged to take him out to lunch at Gravetye.

'Before leaving he once again showed me his books. He was totally blind but knew every book by feel and position on the shelves. He opened a half-bottle of champagne, his daily reviver, and then I eased him into the passenger seat of my Rover 2000 and whizzed through country lanes to Gravetye. I have always been a fast driver and was a bit worried that André, being unable to see, might be worried – but no such thing.

'I was also a bit apprehensive. What would we talk about? Would I be able to keep him amused?

'In the event, he kept *me* amused with a fund of stories and so forth. We had a nice meal. He ate everything put before him and polished off a good bottle of hock and I ran him home, delighted by the experience. I think he enjoyed the outing.'

But the sands were running out. His ninety-third birthday came and went, but his strength was ebbing away. In the summer of 1970 it was clear that the time had come, and it was decided to take him to London and place him in the Middlesex Hospital, where Edith Simon had died. He was under no illusions. As he was carried into his room in the hospital's private wing, he said: 'I know I am going to join my dear wife.'

Still for some weeks he lingered on. A number of old friends went to see him. George Rainbird and Hugh Johnson were regular visitors; one of the last was the much valued Joy Fontes, with whom he talked over happy epicurean occasions of the past. 'As he lay dying,' Mrs Rothwell writes, 'he recalled an evening in Paris, when we had tried to get into the Brasserie Lipp – his favourite – but they were full, so we went to somewhere near, and had oysters and champagne. He couldn't remember the name. It was the Restaurant Calvet, and when I supplied it he seemed so happy, and said "J'ai soif." Those were the last words my friend and mentor said to me.'

The end came in the early hours of 5 September 1970. The last of all his friends to see him alive was his personal physician, Dr Walter Somerville, who visited him on the evening of 4 September. He saw that one wall of the room was lined with cases of champagne, gifts from all over the world. André invited him to open any bottle he liked; he chose a Pommery, and his host remarked that it was the wine that had christened his career in the trade. The dying man was very weak, but Dr Somerville moistened his lips with the champagne and his eyelids flickered. A few hours later he died in his sleep.

Thus did André Louis Simon set out on his last journey.

A few weeks later I received a communication from the Wine and Food Society, to the effect that there would be a memorial Requiem Mass for André Simon in Westminster Cathedral on 19 October 1970. It added that it had been André's wish that a few of his friends should drink a glass of champagne to his memory, and I was accordingly invited to a reception in Westminster Cathedral Hall after the Mass.

When the day came the great cathedral, where André had been for so long a daily attendant, was packed to the doors. The ceremony was moving and impressive. It was very much a family affair. Father Peter Simon, the dead man's Jesuit son, was the celebrant; André *fils* read the lesson, and Sister Madeleine Simon, his youngest child, the bidding prayers. An oration was made by Monsignor Alfred Gilbey, an old friend and member of a family distinguished in the wine and spirit trade. Describing himself as 'the son and grandson of a wine family', Mgr Gilbey said of André: 'To some there may have been an incompatibility between his being co-founder of the Wine and Food Society and the profession of the Christian religion. How long will it be before people appreciate that a proper concern for the material things of life is only elementary gratitude for the Creator?'

The reception was magnificent; nobody who was present is likely to forget it. The 'few friends' who were invited amounted to some four hundred, and they all enjoyed very much more than 'a glass' of champagne. The wine was provided by André *fils*, who was the principal host. Jeanne Rouyer Guillet was of course there, and countless friends of André drank to his health; among them was Marjorie Fletcher, whose connection with the Wine and Food Society had ended a number of years before. Others were George Rainbird, Hugh Johnson, and Victor and Joan Webb. The reception went on until well into the afternoon.

The obituary notices that followed his death paid glowing tribute to the work André had accomplished in the cause of gastronomy. The *Daily Telegraph* called him 'the doyen of wine connoisseurs in Britain and an epicure of world renown'. It quoted Claude Morny, who was now the secretary of the International Wine and Food Society. André Simon, said Morny, 'stimulated English people's interests in better food and wine in the 100 or more books he wrote on the subject. His influence extended to practically every country in the world. He got people to think about what they were eating and drinking rather than just accepting it.'

A tribute which he would particularly have appreciated was paid by Joy Fontes. At the time it seemed easier, explains Mrs Rothwell, to express her feelings in French than in English; 'the French had a word for it.' So she was glad to be asked to contribute to the French journal *Tastevin en Main*. She wrote of her friend: *'C'était un homme remarquable et unique, qui n'a jamais dit que du bien de tout le monde, charmant, courtois, et sa mort sera ressentie avec une peine profonde par les multitudes dans tous les pays cultivés ansi que par ses membres dévoués de* "The International Wine & Food Society" *qu'il a fondé en 1933. Un grand coeur, un grand ami, un grand chrétien, un grand Français, une perte inestimable pour tous.'*

These were immediate tributes. A little later came the memorable obituary article in *Wine and Food*. It was written by George Rainbird, who spoke of André's expertise in the matter of wine; he had never known him wrong about a wine. The article told of his last days, and added:

> To sum up, André was a genius. Wine was his great love, and food to a lesser degree. Letters were also an equal interest and occupation. He wrote many, many books and

hundreds of ephemera. He never stopped writing, even when, at the end of his life, he became blind. He first of all wrote in an enormous script which ran off the page, and he would write on his blotting paper until it was pointed out to him. And then he taught himself to type! Blind, 92, 93, he lived a full life. Indeed, he – as somebody once said about him – 'smoked like a stage Frenchman; he wrote like an angel. He never said a good thing about a bad wine; his memory was fantastic, and his knowledge unique. He had charm and, above all, presence.' He retired from London and was living in his beloved Little Hedgecourt, and in his nineties I have seen him do what I have never seen before or since; he retrieved a claret cork that had got pushed into the bottle, with the aid of a piece of wire.

George Rainbird acclaimed *By Request* as a book that gave 'an insight into the man that was André Simon'. And he ended with the simple words: 'I loved him.'

André Simon is not forgotten. The International Wine and Food Society, as it has been named since 1968, has seen to that. Shortly after his death it was agreed at a Society meeting, on the proposal of Lord Swaythling, that he should be made Perpetual President. A precedent existed in the case of George Saintsbury and the Saintsbury Club. At the same time some of the influential members of the Society were not keen on the idea of having a dead president, and in recent years the title has been tacitly (but not officially) dropped in favour of 'Founder'.

The Requiem Mass and the reception that followed were by no means the last functions organised by the Society in André's honour. Anniversaries have been celebrated on many occasions; the most memorable was the centenary banquet. On 28 February 1977, the hundredth anniversary of the Founder's birth, the Society dined at the Savoy Hotel.

It was a function that had long been planned, partly at least by André himself, who had always hoped that he might be present in person. The dinner was a sumptuous one, and it followed as far as possible the lines laid down by the Founder. The wines were of the first order, culminating in a glass for each diner of Château Latour 1945, one of the truly great clarets of the twentieth century.

One of the hosts of this memorable banquet was André Simon *trois*, grandson of André Louis Simon and son of André *fils* who had himself survived his father by only three years.

Si monumentum requiris, circumspice. The results of the work to which André Simon devoted his life are plain for all to see. That work was carried out first and foremost in England, and English interest in the civilised pleasures of the table has increased out of all knowledge. No longer is English cooking a music-hall joke; English cuisine at its highest can compare favourably with that of any country in the world, with the possible exceptions of France and China. The average Englishman or Englishwoman takes an intelligent interest in what he eats such as was quite unknown to his forefathers of recent date.

As to wine, the improvement is here perhaps even more marked. England has become a nation of wine-lovers, and wine appears on the tables of rich and poor alike. Much of it of course is 'plonk', but plonk itself can have quality. And in the higher circles connoisseurship is equal to that to be found anywhere else in the world.

What applies to Great Britain applies in equal degree to America, to which André devoted much of his attention in his latter years. The United States, with the immense resources of wealth available to the nation, has reached a measure of epicurean appreciation that would have been inconceivable a couple of generations ago.

How much of all this is directly due to André himself cannot be determined. But undoubtedly his influence was great. He was himself a prime example of the truth of the doctrine he preached. For some seventy years he devoted himself to the civilised pleasures of eating and drinking, and the result was that, as he himself testified, he had hardly an ache or pain in his long life. Nobody who remembers his splendid appearance in his old age, his pink-and-white complexion and his air of robust and dignified good health, can have any reasonable doubt of the beneficial effect that his régime of life had on him.

His innumerable literary contributions to gastronomy had incalculable influence. He was the leading epicure of his age, and a catalogue of the developments in the appreciation of wine and food in the twentieth century would be meaningless without recognition of his leadership.

Hugo Dunn-Meynell, now executive director of the International Wine and Food Society, has paid generous tribute to the achievements of his eminent predecessor; it was appropriate that some of his most notable words should have been spoken in a setting that marked the association not only of Britain and France but also of the Old and New Worlds. In 1983 the Society held its convention in Vancouver, and Mr Dunn-Meynell addressed the delegates on the subject: 'Would André be proud of us?'

He traced André's career, and told the story of how the Wine and Food Society came to be formed. Then, in pursuance of his chosen theme, he proceeded:

André's was not in essence a counsel of luxury though he firmly believed that we should enjoy the very best whenever we have the chance. His avowed intention was to persuade people – starting with the members of our Society – to adopt 'more sensible eating and drinking habits'.

Well, the world is much more nutrition-conscious than it was in 1933 – for that we can be thankful. Perhaps some of us err on the side of over-consciousness. I think the fixation of many people about so-called 'health' foods would have amused this man who, in his nineties, was still opening a bottle of champagne at eleven o'clock every morning – and who was able to say shortly before his death that he had 'hardly a pain or an ache in 80 years'.

So, *have* we set an example, and *have* others followed?

Well, for a start, there are thousands of associations in the world devoted to gastronomic appreciation. Some are big, some small. Some local, some national. Some cater for exclusive groups of people, some are open to all comers. But pretty well all of them are based on the principle which André taught. You may think he would approve of that . . .

Our Founder was a pioneer who interested the media in food and drink to a degree never before known . . . On his travels – notably those to this American continent, to Australasia and to Africa – André took an intense interest in the emergent wine industries. He would surely be happy at the superb bottles now coming from farmers in those continents, to whom he gave such encouragement as well as practical advice; and he would indeed be proud that so many of these distinguished new-generation wine makers are members of our Society . . .

Three things I must assert – first, that our Founder would see, in the world today, greater than ever need for an international organisation devoted to maintaining high standards of eating and drinking – and to bringing back some of the traditions of his time that we have so sadly lost. Then, he would have loved the adventurous spirit that is a mark of our Society – trying new foods, working out fresh ways of preparing old ones and sampling unfamiliar wines. And thirdly, that he would be proud to see this great

Vancouver gathering of his loyal supporters and disciples from all over the world . . .

There was more in the same strain, all devoted to the theme of what André had taught and how his teaching had been carried out. Nobody reading Mr Dunn-Meynell's words can question the extent of André's contribution to the cause of civilised living, and therefore to the good of humanity. They may well serve as a suitable epitaph for the great gastronome.

Yet to his friends it was the personality of the man himself, even more than his achievements, that lives in the memory. His geniality was infectious; his whole being was redolent of good nature and warm-heartedness. Anything he could do for others was done with immediacy and enthusiasm, and he was always ready to share the good things of life, which meant so much to him, with as many people as he could. Never was there a kinder man.

It is thus that those of us who had the privilege of knowing him will always remember André Louis Simon.

Index